10-29-56

FREEDOM'S

HOLY LIGHT

FREEDOM'S
HOLY LIGHT

BY

MERRIMON CUNINGGIM

HARPER & BROTHERS PUBLISHERS

NEW YORK

To Whitty

957356

Contents

Preface

You and I have more freedom than we know and than we use. We did not fight to gain it, though many of us have fought to keep it. But military struggles are not the sort to spread its understanding. The best they do is to preserve the chance for freedom's practice in days of peace. Our peace is uneasy, to be sure, but liberty is alive.

Yet it does not always flourish. Nibbles at its edges and bites at its vitals too often go unchallenged. Those who have most to gain from its enhancement, namely, men of firm religious faith, are sometimes least concerned about its infringement. What is lacking? What can help? The answer, I believe, is not so much courage as it is understanding. If we understood more fully the origin and nature of our freedom, we should be better prepared to use it and to value it. In this conviction these pages have been written; in the hope that they may contribute to this understanding they are offered to the public.

My interest in the matters here discussed arose in reverse order to that of the chapters. The origin of my concern was in a dissatisfaction with the alternatives being pressed on us in respect to problems of church-state relations, such as religion in public education, alternatives neither of which represents sound theory or sound practice (Chapter VI). That we are susceptible to such pressure is due to a fairly widespread mis-

understanding of the relationship of church and state, a misunderstanding found even in the thinking of the Supreme Court
(Chapter V). The true relationship, as both history and present
practice show, involves two emphases, one restrictive, one permissive: organic disconnection and sympathetic association of
church and state (Chapter IV).

This problem is one in the general area of religious freedom.
There are two other major aspects: religious liberty at its fullest
calls for the recognition of the supremacy of conscience (Chapter III), as well as, of course, the oft-recognized freedom of
worship (Chapter II). For all three of these aspects of religious
freedom, the actual development in America is strikingly consonant with the desire of the Christian ethic, as I see it (again,
Chapters IV, III and II).

But religious freedom is not neatly separable from other freedoms; moreover, it is not merely one among many. It is the heart
and focus for the rest. America's freedom has religious rootage,
and its central element is *religious* freedom (Chapter I). Even
a brief analysis of religious freedom must therefore begin with
an attention to freedom in general, in all its dimensions (again,
Chapter I). It is my purpose to suggest, on the basis of that
perspective, what our religious freedom consists in, how we
got it, and how we should use it. The last chapter is a bit of a
sermon; how else can one talk about freedom?

The ideas here developed have been discussed in three lecture
series: at Brite College of the Bible, Texas Christian University,
on the Wells Foundation in 1952; at Southwestern University
as the Willson Lectures in 1954; and at Pomona College on the
Clark Foundation in 1955. To all at those institutions who
expressed their interest and friendship, and especially to Presi-

dent M. E. Sadler of T.C.U., President William E. Finch of
Southwestern, President E. Wilson Lyon and Professor John
von Rohr of Pomona, I tender my sincere appreciation.

Others have given counsel and helpful criticism. Those to
whom special thanks are due are William Warren Sweet, Professor Emeritus of both the University of Chicago and Southern
Methodist University; Arthur E. Sutherland, Professor of Constitutional Law at the Harvard Law School; and my colleagues
at Southern Methodist University, Professors Joseph E.
Mathews, Albert C. Outler, Joseph W. Quillian and Decherd
Turner of Perkins School of Theology, and Professor Lennart
Larson of the Law School. They have saved me from errors,
and the faults that remain are mine alone. The person to whom
this volume is dedicated has helped most of all.

MERRIMON CUNINGGIM

Dallas, Texas
May 10, 1955

FREEDOM'S

HOLY LIGHT

CHAPTER I

"Sweet Land of Liberty"

My country, 'tis of thee,
Sweet land of liberty,
Of thee I sing;
Land where my fathers died,
Land of the pilgrims' pride,
From every mountain side
Let Freedom ring.

The Spirit of America

No OTHER phrase sums it up quite so well—"sweet land of liberty." The Star-Spangled Banner sings of "the home of the brave," but first comes "the land of the free." In our Pledge of Allegiance "liberty" precedes "justice for all." And if bravery and justice give place to freedom, so also does equality: according to the Gettysburg Address this nation was "conceived in liberty" before it was "dedicated to the proposition that all men are created equal." Of the qualities of the spirit by which we as a people are or would like to be known, liberty leads all the rest. This is the spirit of America both as we know it in large part and as we would have it known in fuller measure.

We speak of it by either term, "freedom" or "liberty," and in most respects in the political or social order those terms are properly interchangeable. We refer to the "four freedoms" or to our "civil liberties," and with reference to any one of them we are liable to use either word. We say "freedom of conscience" and "religious liberty," "freedom" or "liberty" of the press. The distinction between them is fine: whereas "liberty" commonly calls to mind some previous lack, some restraint in the past, "freedom" more often implies absence of restraint both here and heretofore. In speaking of the natural state of man as God intended him to be, we are more likely to use "freedom"; but in referring to the state of one recently released from slavery, we would probably use "liberty."

Yet seldom would we be so precise. Moreover, the opposites of each are the same: "restraint," "servitude," "repression," "subjection"; or in the other direction, "license," "irresponsibility." With respect to America each is applicable, and each refers substantially to the same practice and the same ideal.

The Testimony of America

These words, too, set the temper of our testimony in intercourse with other nations and other peoples. However often we may fail to rise fully to their expectations of us, they look on us as "the land of the free." Or if by virtue of repeated disappointment in us they have grown cynical, they are still aware that freedom is our symbol, and, sometimes in their eyes, pretense. They felt it appropriate when France's gift of the Statue of Liberty was inscribed with words of welcome to the "huddled masses yearning to breathe free"; and when we adopted various restrictive immigration laws, in spite of our elaborate justifications for them those abroad often looked on them as dilution if not betrayal of our vaunted love of liberty. In the main we have established a record of not seeking a colonial empire, or providing freedom for our colonies when they were ready for it, and of sympathizing with the desires for freedom of subject peoples under the rule of other nations. Whenever we have seemed true to this record, we have received the acclaim and trust of the earth's millions; whenever we have temporized in such policies we have earned their suspicion that we were about to abandon our own high purposes. And in every one of its wars the United States has interpreted its participation as being in some fashion a defense of, or a fight for, freedom, whatever other specific aims were involved. By other nations we deserve to be thought of, and sometimes are regarded, as a generous or brave or imaginative people, but that aspect of our character which our heritage and our influence bring first to their minds is that we are lovers of liberty.

Here is the heart of our national distaste for communism, as we see it embodied in present-day Russia and her satellites. The Curtain between our countries is of Iron, and Russia must continue so to forge it as long as the bonds that encase the individuals within her borders must also be iron. She dare not let her people go free, in speech, in vote, in faith, in personal activity. Much else in her system and her behavior has prompted our general loathing, but it can all be traced to her proscriptions, her restraints, and her slaveries. She is an unmoral scientific laboratory, she is a godless church, but worst of all, she is a jail for the body and spirit of man. Of all the bitter differences between us, our two attitudes toward freedom—her fear and our attachment—is perhaps the crucial factor. Thus it behooves us to use only the instruments of freedom in attacking her position in the world at large or in defending against her infiltration within our own boundaries. We need not use her methods among ourselves or with others, for she cannot succeed as long as America is in fact "sweet land of liberty."

The Confusion of America

Freedom, then, is at the core of America's character and its most influential testimony to the world. And yet we fail to know what it is. We are confused as to its nature, its possibilities and its limits. Variously we call upon its name for support or justification for contradictory points of view and programs. When national holidays come along, we honor freedom with extravagant encomiums. We say we breathe it, we live in it, we die for it. Sometimes it seems we do everything but understand it.

Businessmen are confused. The Far Right claims, in the name of freedom, an economy of complete laissez faire. Just as vociferously the Far Left desires, with its blessings, an industrial machine in large measure owned and controlled by government. The rest of us in the middle know only that we want neither extreme, and are puzzled by the questions: How can the initiative of the individual be preserved, yet necessary controls for the sake of the public good be established? How can we escape the disastrous effects of both cut-throat competition and monopoly? How can the power to make decisions be kept in the hands of the many of a democracy, rather than of the few of an industrial or governmental oligarchy? How can freedom be made productive of both stability and healthy change, rather than of either immovability or chaos? We recognize that our belief in and practice of freedom are at the crux of our economic well-being, but our uncertainty as to the nature of freedom itself leaves us puzzled.

Educators are confused. Here again most of us seek to escape both extremes. We do not believe that freedom in education demands either learning for learning's sake alone, irrespective of its functional aspect, or on the other hand, liberty not to learn. We want our children to undergo the discipline of rigorous study, yet withal to the end that their minds be emancipated, not enslaved. But how? How can both the opportunities and the responsibilities of freedom be effectively shared with the student? How can the teacher play both roles—authority, yet catalytic agent; arbiter, yet counselor? Can education keep from being either indoctrination or indiscipline? Freedom requires an educated citizenry, but how can we teach freedom itself?

Churchmen are uncertain. To the extent to which their puzzlement is concerned with the relationship of religious to governmental organizations—the so-called "separation of church and state"—it constitutes a special problem to be considered in later chapters. But the confusion has to do with other matters as well: the extent of protection a free society should give to conscientious objectors, the right to worship in ways that seem strange to the majority, the duty to allow others such a right. Churchmen as well as educators and businessmen know that the liberty America provides is basic to the furtherance of the interests they profess; but what are the privileges and bounds of this liberty?

Lawyers and politicians are perplexed. For a society such as ours freedom has its necessary counterpart in orderliness— "liberty and justice for all." Yet liberty and justice are in tension with each other as often as they are in partnership, and checks and balances are inescapable when they present conflicting claims. At some point in our history freedom may need to have the upper hand; at another, order. But the past can be viewed with perspective; what about the present? Who is to say which should give ground to the other? Does our phrase, "liberty under law," mean that liberty is subsidiary or fundamental to law? How far does the society put up with the demagogue? On what grounds does it dispense with him? We are convinced that our concept of freedom somehow underlies our definition of legislative, executive, and judicial functions, but what is it that freedom has to say about them?

The Dimensions of Freedom

For clearer guidance through the confusing issues of our day we need a better understanding of freedom. Like motherhood, sunshine and the daily bath, freedom receives the encomiums of everybody from Russian communists to the staunch daughters of respectable revolutions. But "ev'ybody talk about heaven ain't goin' there"; and all of us need to know what freedom really consists in, so that we can discriminate between those whose talk is false and those whose talk is true.

Freedom is not the same as democracy; rather, it subsumes any political arrangement properly called democratic. Therefore we shall not here discuss the various machinery by which democracies function—rule by majority vote, the principle of representation, universal suffrage, the separation of governmental powers, and so on. These and other well-known manifestations of democracy are not so much the essence of freedom as the evidences that freedom has been taken seriously. Consequently we shall center our attention not on the methods of democracy but on the proverbial "rights and duties" of the individual citizen and of the group.

Six aspects of freedom are central. First is the right to express one's opinion openly and to know the opinions of others. Under this heading come both freedom of speech and freedom of the press, about which we hear so much, freedom of access to information, about which we hear perhaps too little, and freedom to petition, which was important enough to be included in our American Bill of Rights, but about which we now hear nothing at all. This general *freedom of expression* has its parallel in the second major aspect, *freedom of action*, which politically means the right to assemble and the right to vote, and beyond political considerations includes the liberty of movement. These first two presuppose the third, *freedom of thought*, and as part of that right, the power to decide. These three—liberty of expression, of action, and of thought—are the freedoms that each man desires for himself, without which he is not a full member of his group.

But if any man demands such rights for himself alone, he means not to live in a free society but to be the governor of an enslaved society. Freedom implies duties as well as rights, and thus it has other meanings that enable it to be socially as well as personally operative. Three more aspects need to be mentioned. Fourth, freedom means *consent*: we need no liberty of thought for the guidance of our expression and action, our speech and our vote, unless we mean to be persuasive with our speech and determinative with our vote. If another is to decide for us, then our freedom is illusory; if not, then we possess freedom in order to join in the making of decisions. As the Declaration of Independence phrased it, governments that mean

to secure liberty derive "their just powers from the consent of
the governed."

The fifth is the necessary partner of the fourth: freedom
means *dissent*. We shall not always be persuasive; others of
contrary opinion will not always succeed in persuading us.
Nor is it merely a matter of persuasion. Democracy at its heart
is a theory of imperfection; it allows itself to be wrong. It
grants to its participants the luxury of controversy, and thus
the even greater luxury of making mistakes. No sane man
would seriously argue that the majority is always right. Right
does not reverse itself as easily as majorities sometimes do. Woe
betide that democracy, then, that forgets that dissent is not
merely a troublesome accompaniment of freedom but part
of the essence. The British phrase "Loyal Opposition" strikes
American ears as strange, but our American brand of freedom,
like the British, knows the soundness in the juxtaposition of
those two words.

Finally, freedom means *concern for the public good:* to the
horror of some present-day pretended defenders of the Constitution, that document states in its Preamble its intention to
"promote the general welfare." As if it were a logical conclusion, the Preamble follows with the aim to "secure the Blessings of Liberty to ourselves and our Posterity." It is a logical
relation: the "blessings of liberty" are illusory when they are
bestowed only on some segment of the population, however
large that segment may be. To protect liberty itself, therefore,
the area of its application must include the whole citizenry.
Freedom calls for the promotion of "the general welfare," or
ends by not being freedom, and not being interested in any-
body's welfare. Imagine how the Pledge of Allegiance would

sound if we sought to set limits on freedom: "I pledge allegiance to the flag . . . one nation, indivisible, with liberty and justice for" some!

But concern for the general welfare, along with but perhaps even more than the other dimensions of freedom, requires an attention to order. Here it is that we see that a social value, order, often taken to be a complement of freedom on the same level, is really a corollary, a deduction from freedom, on a subsidiary level. Order is not an equal value with freedom; certainly it is not contradictory to freedom, requiring that the two always be in tension with each other. The opposite of freedom is not order, but a pair of denials, one in each direction. The true opposites are coercion on the one hand, or on the other caprice.

Now order can hardly be handmaiden to caprice, but it can be party to either coercion or freedom, and must be party to either, if either is to be effective. The difference lies in the aim for which the order is instituted and maintained: order as the accompaniment of coercion is for the sake of making the will of the coercive power supreme, for the sake of coercion; order as the tool of freedom is for the sake of freedom, for the general welfare, as distinct from the welfare of any one individual or group that would invade it. Since it is true that order and coercion are necessary allies, if coercion is to succeed, there may be some justification in our speaking of freedom and order as if they were two separate values. But it behooves us to notice that freedom as much as coercion requires order, that it is a necessary accompaniment of freedom itself, the element that distinguishes freedom from its other true opposite, caprice.[1]

The Religious Aspect

Here, then, we have six major aspects of liberty: freedom of expression, of action, of thought, consent, dissent, and concern for the public good. But something is omitted. One of the items always present in such a listing has not yet been mentioned, namely, *religious freedom*. We cannot discuss, even in brief compass, the dimensions of freedom in America without giving it careful attention.

Yet if all we mean by religious freedom is the liberty to attend services of worship, we have noted it already when we mentioned that freedom involves the right to assemble. Or if all we mean is that a man may believe as he pleases about his God, we have already covered it in freedom of thought. Either we mean something more, or there is no need to give it such special concern.

We do mean something more, so much more as to make it not merely a partner of the other aspects of freedom already referred to, but the basis for all of them. The foundation of freedom is in a religious understanding of man and the universe. Every one of freedom's primary dimensions implies certain assumptions concerning both the nature and destiny of man. Those assumptions, pushed to their extremity, are religious in character; they have to do with the recognition of God or of what man tries to substitute for God. This is not to say that all who accept freedom for what it is are theists, for we know that this is not so. Many of our strongest proponents of freedom, all the way from Thomas Paine to John Dewey, would disagree with the position that the elements of liberty thus far discussed necessarily rest on a theistic base. The point is, rather, that whether or not all the believers in freedom themselves recognize it, the dimensions of freedom imply a foundation that is in truth a religious faith.[2]

There should be inserted at this point a word of warning as to the exact nature of the position here suggested. Much is being said and written these days about the religious, even Christian, foundations of the American Way. Washington has taken up the line, to such an extent as to have provoked the phrase, "Piety along the Potomac," as a characterization of the present political temper. The relationship of religion to government is so asserted as to give the impression that the American Dream and the Kingdom of God are coequal entities; that church and state should engage in mutual blessing; and even that the church member is ipso facto the sound citizen and vice versa.[3] Though some who take such a stand are undoubtedly sincere, the political advantage in such piosities has not escaped others. That all churchmen are by that fact loyal Americans is perhaps a less dangerous *non sequitur* than its contradictory notion, which seemed for a while to attract some Congressional committees. But the whole position that Christianity and America are in some sense synonymous is still a snare and its inevitable partner, a delusion.

Rather, the contention here is that, irrespective of however much or little the institutions of religion should or do recognize and support, or are recognized and supported by, the institutions of government and secular society, the ideals of religion underlie the aspects of freedom; and further, that no other ideals serve as well to substantiate them. Thus the contrary opinions that are being addressed are two, not one, in number: this argument cuts across both that which makes a too-easy identification between the practices of Christianity and democracy, for the support of either, and the other that contends that freedom rests purely on human and secular grounds. Let it be repeated: the dimensions of freedom imply its foundation in a religious faith. It is the position of men who own gladly to such a faith that the Hebrew-Christian tradition more fully and satisfyingly undergirds our freedom than any substitutes can do.

It is not my intention to explore this position fully. Such an exploration would take us into the intricacies of philosophical and theological debate, and lead us away from our appointed task, a consideration of the nature of political freedom, with special reference to religious freedom, as we find it in America today. But though no full-fledged discussion of such matters is here proposed, some passing justification for this position should be given. We shall note briefly the implications of the six dimensions of political and social freedom, taken together. Let it be granted in advance that one or another of the implications finds as hearty support in some secular philosophy of past or present as it does in the Hebrew-Christian tradition; but only in our religious heritage, I believe, do we find all five implications maintained with force and clarity.

First, America's brand of freedom calls for the recognition of the relatedness of all men; and not just a neutral relationship, but one that has in mind the good of each. This is the political-social manifestation of the Hebrew-Christian belief in *brotherhood*. That brotherhood also has its roots in other philosophies goes without saying. The peculiar Hebrew-Christian insistence differs from, say, the Stoic concept in both motivation and desert, and thus finally in derivation. One's "brother" should be loved because love is the first law of life. He is to be loved whether or not he deserves it, and his merit is not simply a self-validating proposition. For it is God who enunciates the law of love; and the admonition to brotherhood is anchored not to man, or to nature and natural law, or to the path of wisdom, but to God as the Jew and the Christian conceive him. Brotherhood is obligatory because all men are children of the one loving Father. Thus does the Hebrew-Christian faith give cosmic support to freedom's premise as to the relatedness of men.

Secondly, no one person's welfare should have precedence over another; the nature of freedom is such as to require the contention that, in some sense, all men are "created equal." But in what sense? On the basis of their measurable worth and dignity? Some protagonists of liberty would have it so, but the argument does not stand up. The plain facts of the human situation convince us that men are not equal in native gifts, or in their capacities for understanding, or for service to the common good, or for discharging any of the duties of citizenship. And yet freedom, flaunting the superficial facts of human difference, calls for some kind of *equality* among men. Secular philosophies stumble and fall in their effort to substantiate such an idea; in the end, many of them throw scorn on it. It is, finally, religion alone that furnishes justification for any such brave position. Religion contends for equality in being, if not in performance; equality in essence, if not in capacity; "created equal"—equality in terms of creation. But to put it in these terms is to put it outside one's self. The mistake in the King James translation of the Hundredth Psalm has a point for us: ". . . It is he that hath made us, and not we ourselves. . . ."[4]

The necessary insistence of freedom on the equality of all men finds its grounding ultimately in religious faith.

These two lead to the third implication. If brotherhood is derivative from fatherhood, and if equality can be maintained only by reference to man's status as a created being, the belief in freedom focuses attention ultimately on his creation and thus on the Creator-Father. Occasionally along freedom's tortuous way some of its supporters have sought to rule God out and set up other gods in his place—see, for example, the French Revolution. But nearly all the great documents of freedom have forthrightly proclaimed that the view of man they enunciated was such as to necessitate the recognition of *man's creatureliness* and of *God's creativity*. Men are "endowed by their Creator with certain unalienable rights," says the Declaration of Independence, and liberty is one of them, an endowment from the hands of God. Lincoln felt that it is "under God" that "this nation . . . shall have a new birth of freedom"; and for most people who look on liberty as something more than rebellion from slavery, love of freedom springs from or eventually entails love for God.

But freedom by itself knows no full-fledged theology, and the religious premises of liberty continue to center attention on man, not on God. The fourth implication has to do with *man's morally dualistic nature*, a position that the Hebrew-Christian tradition has always insisted on. That freedom accepts one side of this dualism, man's goodness, is abundantly clear, for freedom contends that man is capable of governing himself to his own and others' benefit. Thus freedom has sometimes been thought to depend on one or another of the myopic optimisms in philosophy that emphasize only man's power and righteousness. Yet the other side, man's "bent to sinning," as the old hymn phrases it, is also present. Dissent as one of the major dimensions of freedom indicates the recognition of the possibility that error may be pursued by some of the people, and may even prevail, and further, that error as well as truth has its rights. If we disagree, both of us cannot be right; in fact, neither of us may be right. If this disagreement is permissible, as it is in a democracy, then you and I are recognizing that each of us has a right to be wrong. Moreover, it is of the nature of a free society that neither the majority nor the minority can ever have final proof that it is right, and thus can ever legitimately claim it. The Hebrew-Christian phrasing of this insight is that man is both a sinful and a saintly creature; and the conditions of freedom, as distinct from those of either coercion or caprice, affirm this dualistic religious view. Coercion implies that all men are sinners; caprice, that all are saints. Freedom, alone of the three, depends on the realistic Hebrew-Christian view that they are sinners and saints alike.

Finally, the various elements of freedom point to the premise that man is not only free to decide but must exercise the choice that he possesses. The word "freedom" itself implies that man has a measure of free will. And this the Hebrew-Christian tradition also attests, even though it has from time to time flirted with various kinds and degrees of determinism. But something more is meant. The Hebrew-Christian emphasis is not on the mere *possession of free will*, but on its *use*. Man may not pretend to moral neutrality; he must decide. Religion has much to say, of course, about the kind of decisions man should make; but that he must make them is the beginning of its admonition. Freedom's understanding of this religious insight is shown by its going beyond mere allowance of free action to advocacy of it. This insistence on free action is not the contradiction it might at first seem. Liberty in quiescence differs not one whit from slavery, except in its potential for action. It proves its possession of this potential only as it exerts it, that is, as it commits itself, as it acts. The oughtness of each citizen's participation is brought home to us every time we have even such a morally neutral campaign as to register or "get out the vote," and that oughtness has a religious base.

In fact, this moral imperative inherent in freedom can be made to serve as a summary for all five religious implications of freedom. In common parlance we speak of the sense of ought as conscience, and one of the terms we customarily use in any popular analysis of freedom is the phrase *freedom of conscience*. The religious implications of freedom that have been suggested are brotherhood, equality, dependence on God, man's morally dualistic nature, and his need as well as his right to make decisions. All five of these are matters of conscience for the religious man.

Now conscience has to do with a man's faith, his religion. With our eye on freedom of conscience as a summary for these religious implications, let us recapitulate briefly. Freedom demands brotherhood, and the Hebrew-Christian faith demands brotherhood. Freedom believes in equality, and a conscience sensitive to the Hebrew-Christian ethic likewise believes in equality. Freedom points toward, if it does not always confess, a faith in God; it is this belief in God that, for the Jew or the Christian, keeps conscience from being whim. As to man's goodness and sin, it is his religion above all else that saves him both from pretensions of grandeur for his own achievements and feelings of despair for his own shortcomings; that is, that gives him the balanced view of his own nature that freedom demands. Finally, it is again his faith that impels him to "fashion as he feels," to seek to discharge his self-recognized duties to God and neighbor, and thus to his political and social order.

Conscience therefore invades all the premises of freedom, and in its Hebrew-Christian form seems most fully to satisfy the demands of freedom. But note that all along we have been thinking not merely about religious liberty as one aspect of freedom but about all the aspects of freedom together, all six dimensions discussed above. General freedom, the freedom we know in American governmental and social life, is based on a religious conscience and a religious faith. Since the insights of religion are fundamental to all the aspects of freedom—liberty of expression, of action, of thought, consent, dissent, and concern for the common good—religion and freedom are in one sense inseparable, and all freedom is religious freedom. This is the sense in which freedom of conscience can be taken as a sort of summary for general freedom and its implications concerning the nature of man.

But in another and perhaps more limited sense, religious liberty is separable from other types of general freedom. As the phrase is commonly used, religious freedom has to do with specific liberties related to a man's or a group's conscious religious allegiance. It is with respect to religious freedom of this narrower definition that the discussion will be conducted in succeeding chapters. But the point to note now is that the relationship between freedom and religion that has been suggested indicates that religious freedom in this limited sense is the mainspring of all the other freedoms, not merely the partner but the foundation of all the rest that freedom means. Because all freedom is in one sense religious freedom in general, then in a narrower connotation religious freedom in particular is the heart of general freedom. Religious liberty, in general or particular, is *the liberty to take one's religion into full account, in thought, expression, and action, for one's own and the common good.*

The Roots of Freedom

Do we find that this undergirding concept of religious liberty is recognized in the history of the struggle for freedom? What are the roots of liberty? From what soil sprang the ideas of, and the movements for, freedom of thought and expression, the necessity for consent and dissent, and all the rest? Did religious faith consciously enter into these ideas and movements? Did those who spoke on behalf of their religious faith play a determinative role in the struggle? Was the religious aspect of liberty recognized as paramount? Beyond that, did religion, through the voices of its spokesmen, sanction the development of political and social freedom? We shall examine these questions briefly.

The history is confused. Yet through all the pull and shove of the centuries some clear and prevailing tendencies have been discerned by students of the process. First of all, we know in the main those to whom we are in debt for the origin and spread of freedom in the Western world. We give homage to Aristotle's conceptions and the practices of the Greek city-states, to the philosophy of the Stoics and the record of the Roman Republic. Yet for all the concepts and practices that were worked out in those ancient days, the period of the Dark and

Middle Ages put an effective stop to the growth of democratic thought and life; and the history of what we know as freedom begins almost afresh with the Renaissance. Life became more humane and leisurely, wealth increased, education flourished, scientific inquiry developed, and these things made the despotisms of church and state less tolerable. It is true that the short-range result of the Renaissance and even of the Reformation was to confirm the practice of autocracy, but the spirit of liberty had reappeared, perhaps in stronger fashion than ever before in human history, and democracy was on the march.[5]

Seventeenth century England has often been called the birthplace of modern democracy. The English had their Magna Carta and the traditions of the common law as a starting point, but Tennyson to the contrary, it was not a case where "freedom slowly broadens down from precedent to precedent." In two important instances, the Cromwellian Rebellion and the Revolution of 1688, freedom skipped some precedents in England of the seventeenth century. These great events in the history of man's struggle for freedom, one largely abortive, the other largely successful, found their justification in the political philosophy of John Locke. In contrast to Hobbes's picture of man's life as "solitary, poore, nasty, brutish and short," an interpretation that persuaded Hobbes to defend absolute authoritarianism,[6] Locke trusted man, believed in his capacity for, and right to, self-government, and viewed the state as properly depending only on consent.[7] He was thus an exponent of freedom in many of the ways in which we know it, and his philosophy served not only as justification for the Puritan Rebellion, which he intended, but also as explanation and charter for what took place in the succeeding years among English-speaking peoples. When Marlborough and the British Navy soon managed to defeat Louis XIV and the French, the belief that freedom was necessarily weaker than despotism was successfully challenged.[8] Those who first shaped the ideals of our American brand of liberty—Jefferson, Madison, Thomas Paine, the framers of the Constitution—were disciples of John Locke and students of English history.[9] More than to any other one nation or period we owe our concept of freedom to the men and events of seventeenth century England.

The Religious Sanction

But to answer our questions we need to go back and trace another strand of influence. Many a writer on this theme has shown us that the roots of freedom rest not alone in Athens and the Rome of the Stoics, but also in Jerusalem and the Rome of the Christians. For Jew and Christian saw man as a child of God, and the equality of all men in the sight of God. They saw brotherhood as a reality and thus an obligation imposed on all men, and they asserted the moral responsibility of each individual. Yet these premises for our political freedom lay largely dormant through the Dark and Middle Ages, even as did the insights of the Greeks and Romans. Nor did the Reformation use them consistently in the direction of creating what we think of as religious liberty. Luther's testimony is confused, for though he spoke for freedom against the Roman Church, he spoke for something less than freedom in support of the German princes. Other reformers were similarly ambiguous; and the positions of churchmen, both Catholics and Protestants, have been variable, to such an extent that historic Christianity as an institution in society has appeared to be as often an enemy of freedom as a friend.[10]   957356

But the picture clears up somewhat, at least for Protestants, the further we move from the Reformation; and the influence of religion on the development of freedom is seen quite vividly in the arena in which our ideas of liberty were first successfully maintained, namely, seventeenth century England. The embryonic form of the argument that Locke made so forcefully in his *Treatises on Civil Government* is the work of the English churchman Richard Hooker, of the preceding century, in his *Laws of Ecclesiastical Polity*. Locke carried Hooker's ideas further than Hooker himself would have approved; but one of Locke's key contentions, that government must rest on public approbation, came directly from Hooker, and Hooker got it from his understanding of the nature of moral man and the foundation of morality in the laws of God.[11] Hooker's ideas were not well regarded in his own day, but as we enter the period of overt struggle for political liberty we find another great churchman calling consciously on his religious faith to buttress his concern for freedom. John Milton, in his *Areopagitica* and other prose works, bases his passionate pleas for various civil liberties on his contention "that all men naturally were born free, being the image and resemblance of God himself. . . ."[12] Under the influence of Milton and others, the Puritans rallied to freedom not only because they needed it but also because they saw it as the will of God.

Hooker and Milton helped to shape John Locke. But what about Locke himself? He too argues for the religious base of all liberty and specifically for religious liberty; for freedom rests in natural rights and natural rights stem from God.[13] In spite of the fact that many who fought against the tide of freedom were churchmen, and brought their religion in to support their struggle, the weight of those who spoke in the name of religion came more and more to shift to the side of freedom. What is perhaps more important, the proponents of liberty, whether or not they were known primarily as churchmen, whether or not they were strong defenders of the faith, came more and more to recognize the religious aspect of freedom in general. Religious faith was seen as the sanction of liberty, and religious liberty, freedom of conscience, as the fountainhead of all the other liberties.[14]

Yet we must not exaggerate the scope of the pre-American development. Hooker, Milton, and Locke tended the soil, but their writings suggest that no one of them would have been prepared for the flower of freedom as it has grown in America. For example, nothing in the thought of any one of the three would lead us to suppose that he would have accepted what we have come to call the "separation of church and state." But this is simply to say that they were necessarily children of their own time and place, and the enlargement and extension of their ideas were possibilities with which they themselves did not have to deal.

Their contributions to the growth of freedom have been so thoroughly treated elsewhere that no detailed analysis is called for here.[15] Reference is made to them simply to point out the fact that they support the idea of the religious nature of freedom, to the extent to which this was understood when our national forms and traditions were first established. Thus their work contributes to the conviction that religious freedom is the focus for all the rest of freedom's elements, the key to understanding the nature of the liberty that is ours.

This brief examination of both the dimensions and the historical rootage of freedom suggests that Sidney Smith was using his words carefully when he sang,

> Long may our land be bright
> With freedom's holy light.

For freedom's light is not merely human, man-made, secular; it is a holy thing, rooted in religious faith. To understand more fully the nature of this freedom as we developed it and know it in America, so that we may turn our confusion about it into appreciation for this "sweet land of liberty," we must now give ourselves to a fuller exploration of its keystone element, religious freedom, and of that element's component parts.

CHAPTER II

Freedom to Worship

Religious Freedom Is a Reflex

THOSE of us who go to church on Sunday morning do so with no thought as to the possibility that we may be interfered with or turned aside. We go because we believe or are struggling to believe, because we possess a conscious religious faith or are seeking one, or perhaps something of the two together.

Both the doubt and the assurance that impel us to church are matters between us and God; and if it never occurs to us that someone might prevent our attendance at church, certainly it is impossible for us to conceive of any effort being made to censor the inner workings of our minds and hearts. Now there are all kinds of frivolous reasons for our going to church, but we usually know that they are frivolous; and the underlying and serious motive, no matter how often you and I may betray it in our own personal practices, is to worship God, to find his will for our lives, to express our faith in him. And so we proceed to our local congregations of a Sunday morning, free to do so, and secure in the knowledge of that freedom.

And when we get to the sanctuary the doors are open. It doesn't occur to us that they might be closed. We join with others in passing through those doors, and in standing, sitting, and kneeling, as the forms of our common worship call for. Some of our associates are strangers to us, but no one stopped them at the entrance; in fact, sooner or later they are invited to be strangers no longer. Most of us are regular communicants, and we make up the membership of an institution that is highly organized, with local chapters and national offices. Not only are we free to attend, but the church to which we belong is free to exist, to invite our attendance, to set the terms of our membership, to conduct its various affairs as its own constitution determines—and we take all this for granted.

We even take for granted that the doors of the rival and similar institution down the street will also be open, and that there will be some who will direct their steps to that sanctuary. We make no protest about this, for without giving it a thought we know that those people have the same liberty to attend, and that that church has the same right to exist, that we assume for ourselves and our church.

Within our sanctuary we worship, and one of the results is that our consciences are stirred. Sometimes this pricking of the bubble of our own egotism and complacency results in a changed attitude and a renewed purpose within us; but such redirection of our thoughts cannot be altogether personal, that is, cannot fail to have at least some social manifestations. At other times the stirring of our consciences has more immediately and directly social repercussions. As a result of our worship we see our society as well as ourselves in a new light, and we may be moved to testify in some public way to this clearer vision we gain. Moreover, we know that this happens to those around us as well as to ourselves, and that this is a normal and desirable result of our corporate worship together.

Most of the time, perhaps, our consciences do not get us into trouble. We determine to love our brother more fully, to deal more honestly with our associates, to play a more unselfish role in our family and community life—and all these manifestations seldom cause any difficulty for us, or for those around us. We assume we have the liberty to direct our actions according to such impulses if we have the will to do so.

But some people do not have as good control over their consciences as we do; and we can imagine that, if not for ourselves, at least for others, the following of the dictates of conscience, the responding to the voice of God as it is heard in one's worship, might make trouble in the social scene. Non-meat-eaters, non-flag-saluters, non-war-fighters, non-monogamists, these and others, we can understand, declare that their actions are based on insights gained from their worship, even as our socially less provocative ones are. As long as such actions do have their origin in religious faith, most of us have sympathy for their position, yet are withal puzzled as to how far their unusual behavior should be allowed to go. Thus there arises at this point some uncertainty in our minds as to the proper limits of free response to what one takes to be the voice of God; but in the main you and I bump up against such people only occasionally.

And so the ease with which we assume that we and others have full freedom to respond to the demands of our consciences as the result of our worship of God, is seldom disturbed by the realization that a problem might exist in this area for a few citizens. Here as before, we have all the liberty we need, and we can hardly imagine it otherwise.

Now this is religious freedom, and in its various possible ramifications, in the demands our consciences may make on us in all areas of our living, we can see that it is the heart of our general liberty, the focus for our various other liberties. These are its components: we can believe as we please, worship as we please, and respond to our consciences almost as we please. Moreover, we grant those same rights to others, with very few —though puzzling—exceptions. Furthermore, we can associate with each other in such manifestations of our faith, we can form churches and synagogues, and can support them in their social testimonies, without suffering any civil disabilities thereby. Finally, this freedom—and here is one place at which we need to be mindful of the close distinction between "freedom" and "liberty," for this is full-fledged freedom, the absence of restraint, not mere liberty, the overcoming of restraint—this freedom is so much a part of us that it has become reflex. We do all this without thought. This is normal behavior for America and for church-going Americans.

Questions and Propositions about Religious Freedom

Yet it was not always thus, even in the "land of the free." If we had a close eye to the historical development, we might more properly speak of it after all as religious liberty rather than religious freedom. When we are confused about freedom in other areas, it is not good enough for us blithely to continue in the assumption that the area of religious freedom is trouble-free. In order to understand and exercise our religious freedom fully we need to know both what is desirable and what is actual. What do we want? Why do we want it? What have we got? How did we get it? How closely parallel are the desirable condition and the actual situation? When armed with answers on these matters, where do we come out?

It is to such questions as these that we shall henceforth turn our attention. But first a word must be said as to how the two terms "desirable" and "actual" are being used. "Desirable" is not meant to suggest that all of us desire one particular brand, or interpretation, of religious freedom. Not all Americans think alike on this, any more than on any other subject. Here the "we" is being used in a limited sense, to refer to Christians. Yet even we Christians are by no means in actual unanimity. The suggestion is, rather, that a conscientious inspection of the principles of Christian social ethics leads to certain conclusions in this area. Uncertainties in the application of the Christian ethic will of course abound, but the certainties are sufficiently large and clear to be instructive. In other words, the Christian ethic desires a general kind of religious freedom.

We Christians must not be pettily exclusive about our liberty-loving premises; on examination we shall discover that in most particulars our Jewish friends desire the same arrangements, based on a similar ethic. Nor must we Christians suppose we are of one general mind; Catholics will not agree with everything here to be suggested, and there will also be some Protestant disaffection. But for all of that, the Christian ethic, it is submitted, speaks with remarkable clarity on the points at issue; and the word "desirable" is used to refer to what that ethic calls for, whether Jews also agree or some Christians disagree.

By "actual," reference is made to what is current in the United States. Thus the use of the first person plural pronoun here is not subject to the restriction noted above. With reference to what we possess, the "we" has a broader base: it is meant to sum up all of us who are Americans, regardless of our religious

faith or lack of it. Yet the "actual" in respect to religious freedom, as it shall be described, may not accurately reflect, in
literal fact, every situation in the United States now. Again,
our national practice is too diverse to allow for such over-
simplification. The suggestion, rather, is that the status to be
termed "actual" is in the main the existing interpretation and
practice. Further, it is maintained that the history of the development of religious freedom in this country justifies and
supports these prevailing practices, and calls in question the
propriety of their opposites whenever they exist.

While I am about it, let me make a clean breast of a further
thesis involving the two terms "desirable" and "actual." My
contention is that with respect to the character of religious
freedom in America, there is a striking parallelism—though by
no means an exact identity—between the actual and the desirable. We Americans now have, or have available, what most
Protestants, plus many Jews and some Catholics, want, or ought
to want. Yet we do not fully realize that we have it or that we
want it. In the much too brief analysis on which we are about
to embark, the excuse for submitting these propositions lies not
in their newness, for many scholars have examined various ones
of them in exhaustive fashion, but in their being marshaled
together, and in the conclusions to which their being related
leads us. To put it another way, your author is not only head-
strong but multidextrous—he is climbing out on three limbs at
one and the same time: first, a suggestion as to the type and
extent of the religious freedom that the Christian ethic desires
or calls for; second, a suggestion as to the actual character of
religious freedom as we have known and know it in America;
and third, a proposition that the desirable and the actual are

very close together. On the basis of this presentation a conclusion will be offered as to how all this is related to our
present-day concerns in various fields, with some hints as to
what we ought to do about it.

To divide our subject into manageable proportions, we shall
consider three aspects of religious freedom, all of which are
reflected in our habits of a Sunday morning. First, we go to
church. Thus we need to understand both what is desirable
and what is actual as to the *freedom of personal worship*.
Second, God speaks to our consciences. Thus we must know
to what extent we as religious people believe in and we as
citizens recognize the *supremacy of conscience*. Finally, we
worship and act not as individuals alone but as members of
ecclesiastical groups whose liberty, in whatever measure it
exists, is a facet of our own. Thus we must examine both the
desirable and the actual *relationship between church and state*
to discover the way in which they should be and are related to
each other. Many other matters are involved in religious freedom, but they can all be subsumed under these three: freedom
of worship, supremacy of conscience, and the relationship of
church and state. To the first of these we shall confine ourselves
in the remainder of this chapter.

The Demand of the Christian Ethic

The Christian understanding of the nature of man calls for
the recognition that he should be free to worship God as his
conscience, enlightened and disciplined, dictates to him. This is
the first half of the position; the counterpart is: A man must
grant to his neighbor the privilege he claims for himself. The
two go together in the Christian understanding, though by

nature we are so self-centered as seldom to have arrived at the
second, either in theory or in practice, except by way of the
first.

Now we should not expect to find that our present-day interpretation of this or of any other social principle springs full-
blown, and in twentieth century terminology, from the thought
of Jesus or of the early church. We are aware that the condition of men and the shape of the world force on us the continual reassessment of the moral and spiritual values in which
we believe, and their continual reapplication to the changing
scene. This is necessary in order to keep our faith pertinent and
vital, and true in spirit to the original fount. Thus of necessity
we shall eschew the proof-text method of reading the Bible,
and shall seek rather to understand the prevailing temper of the
Old and New Testaments. Similarly, modern scholarship has
shown the pitfalls in appealing to Jesus directly; our references,
rather, should be understood as being addressed to the memory
of Jesus current in the Christian community. The reader will
recognize the difficulty in making such a distinction each time
Jesus is referred to; and the writer will proceed to refer to
him, rather than to communal recollection, in the hope that
the effort being made to catch the atmosphere of the man and
his times will be held in mind.

Yet we must be careful lest, in testing the temper, we read
modern presuppositions into the thought patterns of ancient
days. Nor must we, on the other hand, fail to listen to the
central testimony their writings sought to convey, for this
testimony concerning God and, for the New Testament,
God in Christ, colored all their thinking on subsidiary subjects.
Their premises are often not America's, and we must not make

the mistake of supposing that they are. Moreover, their ideas were seldom systematized, and we would play them false by building systems out of them. Thus our method here, and in the parallel sections in succeeding chapters, must be that of inquiry into the mind of that time, to seek to sense its direction, and then that of translation into our different age, to catch the hints of where such a direction would now lead us.

Armed with these cautions, we still proceed to suggest that freedom of worship, as we use the phrase, is in consonance with the spirit of Jesus, as we are given to understand it, and with much of the Hebrew tradition of which he was heir. Freedom of worship turns on those two key words: man in essence is free, and man must worship. This is not the paradox it might seem. Man possesses some measure of choice, of free will; and man's proper duty is to exercise that choice by worshiping God. The ground of freedom, therefore, is in the character of God. God desires devotion, but devotion cannot be forced. Freedom is necessary in order to enable man to adopt the filial rather than the frightened relationship with God that God desires.

Jesus seemed to assume such propositions because of the contributions of his predecessors in the long line of Hebrew prophets and writers. These insights did not come easily to the children of Israel, for buffeted by the outrageous fortunes of the centuries, they played around from time to time with deterministic notions and false idols. Yet through it all there developed the strains of thought that contended for the recognition of both freedom of choice and personal obligation to love God. One of the basic meanings of the Creation story is that man could choose, and often did so to his harm. And the work of

the prophets, particularly of Jeremiah and of Ezekiel, resulted
in a growing awareness of the inwardness of religion, and the
moral responsibility of the individual. Joshua's challenge to the
nation was, "Choose you this day whom you will serve," and
Jeremiah and Ezekiel made it a challenge to the individual as
well as to the group.[1]

All this Jesus inherited, for he took his stand firmly in the
line of the Hebrew prophets. Thus one must not think of such
insights as exclusively Christian, for the Jew also has claim on
them and owes allegiance to them. It was as a good Jew of the
prophetic stream that Jesus believed that God had given man at
least a measure of choice, and that each individual must choose,
and by implication must be free to choose. As a metaphysic,
behaviorism of any sort, ancient or modern, finds no authentica-
tion in Jesus' thinking. Man possesses choice, and there is an
obligation on him to exercise it. The prodigal may stay with the
pigs or go home to his father; the priest, the Levite, and the
Samaritan may stop to administer aid or pass by on the other
side; the prostitute may continue her self-defeating life or may
go and sin no more; Peter and the rest of the disciples may affirm
or deny the revelation vouchsafed to them.[2]

Yet Jesus did not thereby believe in religious license. He
sought not to set every man loose to follow his own whimsical
bent, but to readjust the thoughts and patterns of worship and
of daily living so as to allow the individual to breathe fresh air
through them. He said it better: "I have come not to abolish
but to fulfill." The freedom in which Jesus believed carried
with it the awesome obligation to take into account the experience and wisdom of others, as represented by the Law.[3] Only
"Love God and neighbor," not the Law, was the final authority;

and that could not be made fully external and legalized. Yet the Law was urgent advice, and man's proper balancing of freedom and obligation would result in his giving it large credence.

How does this general trend of thought apply to our specific problem? If Jesus were to be suddenly transported to our society, knowing naught of our mores, it is unlikely that he would see the full implications of his ideas for our situation. This is not to suggest, of course, that we see further or more clearly than he did; it is merely to say that in his enunciation of general principles he did not pretend to prescribe detailed social solutions for societies other than his own. But whatever would have been Jesus' attitude to such a society as ours, it is clear that his immediate and many of his more distant followers did not interpret his principles as Protestant Christians now do. For example, Paul talks a great deal about liberty, particularly in his Epistle to the Galatians, but it is the spiritual freedom "wherewith Christ hath made us free," an altogether inner state that could as easily be antagonistic to as sympathetic with freedom of worship as it is here being used.[4] Paul's interpretation not only could be but has been antagonistic, and on the whole the record of Christian history does not support us.[5]

But the rudiments of Christianity's present position on freedom of worship are unmistakably present in the thought and spirit of the prophets, and especially of Jesus as the early church remembered him. A man's religion must be his own, not an easy appropriation of someone's else; he must cry with the Psalmist of old, "O God, thou art my God." If it is to be his own, he must make conscious choice of it. If he must make conscious choice, the choice must be real—that is, other choices must actually be available to him. He must have liberty to choose what to him seems to be the nature of the God whom he would worship, and thus what seems the proper mode of worshiping his God. And lest this choosing be real only for himself, he must grant the same measure of choice to others. It is in some such fashion as this that present-day Christians and Jews, with very few exceptions, conceive of freedom of worship. And because these ideas are so closely parallel to their Biblical counterparts, the Hebrew-Christian position today seems to be that, no matter the various restrictive positions of Christian leaders and congregations through the years in different societies, freedom of worship as that phrase is here being used is alone consonant with the ethic of the prophets and of Jesus.[6]

The American Heritage

To determine the extent to which the demand of the Christian ethic is met by the American actuality, we must look to the sources of our life in the history of this nation. Examination of the earliest years of that history do not give us much assurance, for we discover that there was not a single one of the original thirteen colonies in which freedom of worship was consistently and fully practiced. To those of us who learned the colonial story as an outgrowth of our grade school observance of Thanksgiving, this information may come as something of a shock. Dressed in what we took to be Pilgrim garments, we paused long enough in our enactment of the landing on Plymouth Rock—or more probably in our pasting of pumpkins, turkeys, and tomahawks on the schoolroom windows—to learn that the Pilgrims came to these foreign shores to escape oppression and to be able to worship God as they pleased. "This," said our teacher, "is why we can go to the Methodist, or Catholic, or Episcopalian, or any other church we want to,"—and we ran home from school that day with a nice, warm feeling inside.

But our teacher was wrong. The Pilgrims, and particularly the settlers of Massachusetts Bay Colony, would not have put up with Methodists, or Catholics, or Episcopalians. It is true that they did not want anyone else to tell them how to worship God, but they did want to tell others. They wanted freedom for themselves, but they were not prepared even to tolerate those who differed from them.[7] The Puritans of the Massachusetts settlements imposed all manner of restrictions on dissenters, and persecuted even to the death people whom they considered to be heretical.[8] Because we successfully escaped from grade school, we went on to learn about the banishment of Anne Hutchinson and Roger Williams, and the hanging of Quakers on Boston Common. The thing to be particularly noticed is that such incidents were not merely lapses from the high ideal of tolerance that the Puritans had set themselves, but were in conformity with what they conceived to be the virtue of intolerance.[9] Their practice on these notorious occasions was not in conflict with their theory, for they simply did not believe in freedom of worship.

Yet we should not point our finger of disapproval only at Massachusetts. Though there is no record of capital punishment for religious views in any other colony, lesser measures were often used and restrictions against free worship were general. Some groups in particular were anathema—Jews, Catholics, Quakers, and others—though the extent of the limitations they suffered varied from colony to colony, depending on the size of the dissenting group and the temper of the times. Whether the majority were Congregationalists in Connecticut, Dutch

Reformed in New Netherlands and New York, Presbyterians in New Jersey, or Anglicans in Virginia and the Southern colonies, the point of view was not dissimilar to that of the Puritans of Massachusetts: the worship of God by those who were out of step with that majority was not a right, and often not even a privilege; and the communities set up their restrictive laws and customs accordingly.[10]

Even in Rhode Island, Maryland, and Pennsylvania, justly famed for the large measure of toleration they allowed at various times, the full extent of religious freedom was not attained. If the ideas of Roger Williams had been consistently followed, perhaps Rhode Island would have succeeded, for he showed in his writings, particularly in his famous pamphlets in the controversy with John Cotton, a passionate belief in freedom of worship.[11] His actions supported his words, for under his leadership and that of John Clarke Rhode Island became a refuge for those from other colonies who were oppressed for their religious views. "Forced worship," he once wrote, "stincks in Gods nostrils."[12] But though Rhode Island remained true to his ideals throughout the seventeenth century, the colony later placed certain civil disabilities on Catholics and Jews.[13]

Maryland and Pennsylvania similarly developed their reputation for tolerance on the basis of the views of an outstanding champion of liberty in the leadership of each colony. Cecil Calvert, the second Lord Baltimore, is justly known for the Act of Toleration of 1649; and though he never visited his colony he succeeded in setting up policies that enabled Protestants and Catholics to live together in relative harmony for a considerable period of time.[14] When Protestants finally gained full control, however, restrictive measures were instituted against the Catholics in Maryland.[15]

As for Pennsylvania, William Penn set such an excellent example of Christian charity in the Great Law of 1682 and in other writings and actions that his colony came to be a haven for a wide variety of persecuted groups—Lutherans, Mennonites, including the Amish, Moravians, Schwenkfelders, and others.[16] He ordained that no person shall "be compelled to frequent or Maintain anie religious worship, place or Ministry whatever, Contrary to his, or her mind, but shall freely and fully enjoy his, or her, Christian Liberty in that respect, without any Interruption or reflection."[17] Yet even there political privileges were limited to Christians; and before the Revolution and as a result of British pressure Catholics were not allowed to hold public office.[18]

These three great champions of tolerance—Roger Williams, a Baptist, Cecil Calvert, a Catholic, and William Penn, a Quaker—are worthy to stand in the same company with John Milton and John Locke as seventeenth century leaders in the fight for liberty. Through their influence a liberalizing spirit began to grow in all the colonies during the eighteenth century. Moreover, other factors aided this development. Some having to do directly with religion were the multiplicity of religious sects, the rapid growth of dissenting groups, the varied experiences of the colonies with respect to established churches (to which reference will be made in Chapter IV), the opposition to nonresident bishops and later to the possibility of resident bishops, and the results of the Great Awakening throughout the colonies and in all Protestant groups.[19] Secular influences were the effect of the English Revolution of 1688, the existence of a large non-church membership in the colonies, the spread of deism among the educated people, the migration of the colonists from one part of the country to another, and the growing importance of foreign trade.[20]

But in spite of all these movements, the most that can be said for the situation on the eve of the Revolution is that a large measure of toleration in the matter of religious worship had grown up. And toleration is not religious liberty. Though a man's peculiar worship may be tolerated, yet if he suffers some civil disability because of it he does not possess full freedom in that regard. And this was still the status, in varying degrees, in every one of the colonies at the outbreak of the Revolutionary War.[21]

The first blow for religious liberty of the full type, as distinct from mere toleration, was struck in Virginia in the year of the Declaration of Independence. The ground had been well prepared in preceding years by the work of the rapidly growing dissenting groups, largely Presbyterians and Baptists, led by such men as Samuel Davies, a Presbyterian, who remonstrated against the restrictions of the established Anglican Church.[22] Their protests were supported by such loyal Anglicans as James Madison, whose horizons had been broadened by his attendance at the Presbyterian college of Princeton, and by such nominal Anglicans as Thomas Jefferson, who had drunk deep of John Locke and the deists. The result of this combination of forces was the passage of the famous Virginia Bill of Rights in 1776.

An examination of this Bill indicates the importance of the distinction between toleration and liberty. The Bill, drafted by Patrick Henry, in his version included the clause:

that all men should enjoy the fullest toleration in the exercise of religion according to the dictates of conscience, unpunished and unrestrained by the magistrate, unless under color of religion any man disturb the peace, the happiness, or safety of society.[23]

But Madison objected to the word "toleration," and the clause was stricken out. Madison said,

> Toleration belonged to a system where was an established church, and where a certain liberty of worship was granted, not of right, but of grace; while the interposition of the magistrate might annul the grant.[24]

Thus by taking exception to a term hitherto well-regarded, Madison made possible the creation of a new and higher conception of religious freedom. The final version of the Bill read:

> That religion, or the duty that we owe our Creator, and the manner of discharging it, can be directed only by reason and conviction, and not by force or violence; and that, therefore, all men are equally entitled to the full and free exercise of religion, according to the dictates of conscience; and that it is the mutual duty of all to practice Christian forbearance, love and charity towards each other. No man, or class of men, ought on account of religion to be invested with peculiar emoluments or privileges, nor subjected to any penalties or disabilities, unless under color of religion the preservation of equal liberty and the existence of the State are manifestly endangered.[25]

Later that same year penalties on dissenters were removed by the General Assembly, and Virginia had assumed the role of leader in the establishment of full freedom of worship in the new nation-to-be.

Some of the other states, notably North Carolina and New York, were not far behind. By the time of the Constitutional Convention in 1787 nearly all the states had prepared new constitutions, and in the majority of them significant steps were taken toward the institution of full freedom of worship.[26] Virginia merits special attention, because it was that state that served as a model for the other states and for the new Federal Government. What happened first in Virginia happened in other places, soon or late; and full religious liberty, universally absent in colonial days, came eventually to be the theory and practice of the whole nation.

Since many state constitutions were already settling the question, and since it was felt that matters of religion should properly be in state rather than Federal hands, the only attention given to the problem in the Federal Constitution was in Article VI, paragraph 3, the prohibition of religious tests for Federal offices.[27] In the Bill of Rights, adopted in 1791, it was specifically provided as part of the First Amendment that "Congress shall make no law . . . prohibiting the free exercise" of religion. Though these two provisions did not bind the states, they were fully in consonance with the spirit of the Virginia enactments, and effectively influenced the states still lagging behind to take necessary steps to insure freedom of worship within their borders.[28]

The American Fact

What has happened since has been simply a broadening of the understanding and application of the religious freedom that was secured in Virginia, then in the other states and the Federal Government. In colonial America it took time to proceed from a situation in which worship contrary to the practice of the majority was prohibited, to one in which it was handicapped, and finally to one in which it was tolerated. Similarly,

it has taken time for us to digest the full implications of the
new freedom of worship that went beyond mere toleration.
One important step along the way was the famous action
Marbury v. Madison in 1803;[29] for John Marshall's bold decision that the Constitution was supreme over any legislative
action meant that its provisions affecting religious freedom, as
well as affecting other matters, were not subject to change by
the passage of some contrary law.[30] Another important step
was the Fourteenth Amendment, ratified in 1868, which provided that

> No state shall make or enforce any law which shall abridge the
> privileges or immunities of citizens of the United States; nor shall
> any State deprive any person of life, liberty, or property, without
> due process of law. . . .

The significance of this Amendment for religious liberty has
only been seen in fairly recent times, as its clauses have been
construed by the Supreme Court to embody the various provisions of the Bill of Rights and to prevent state actions inconsistent with them. By several recent decisions the Court has
affirmed that the states as well as Federal Government may not
prohibit the free exercise of religion.[31]

It is thus that we in America have come to enjoy a freedom
to worship God as we will. Many particular problems remain,
some of which we shall refer to in later chapters. But the
general dimensions of that freedom are secure for ourselves
and our fellows of whatever religious persuasion. Thus in
concluding the discussion of this aspect of our religious
liberty, we need merely to call attention briefly to three facts
that have been involved in the story. First, this freedom to
worship was brought about in large part by men of religious

faith, in the name of their understanding of that faith. This is what we would have expected, but their struggle was against men also of religious faith; and perhaps that is not altogether what we would have expected. An effort to develop the significance of this realization will be made in Chapter V. Secondly, the achievement was a boon, not a blow, to religious people. Contrary to the fears of some and the hopes of others, the enactments in Virginia and later elsewhere served, as Anson Phelps Stokes has well said, "not as a protection *from* religion, but rather as a protection *for* religion."[32] And finally the actual situation with respect to freedom of worship is almost identical with the desirable status in the light of present-day understandings of the Christian ethic. We may well cherish what we have in America, for our faith, rooted in the Hebrew-Christian tradition, tells us that it is good.

CHAPTER III

The Supremacy of Conscience

The Problem of Conscience

THE second aspect of religious freedom is closely related to the first. Worship is no one-way street; in it we speak to God, but God also speaks to us. Worship is of course adoration, praise, thanksgiving, and it is also something more: it is the conscious exposure of one's life and thought to God. Thus it is confession, penitence, and commitment. If our worship rises to this level, things are likely to get embarrassing. When we recognize our sin, it is in the light of some divine standard over against which we have come to see our own failures and shortcomings. When we repent of our sin, it is because we would through God's grace be released from its bondage. And when we dedicate ourselves anew to his righteous way, it is with the prayer that he grant that we may ever thereafter "serve and please" him "in newness of life, to the honor and glory" of his holy Name.

Then what is God's will for us? We strive to understand it, and gain insights from the struggles of his saints through the centuries. Christians find in Jesus Christ the revelation not only of the character but of the will of God, and thus we seek to understand his life, his thought, and his nature. This we do

58

in order to consecrate our total beings—which includes our actions—more fully to him. We strive, we seek, we find. Or, more accurately put, we are apprised; God finds us. God searches us out. God lays bare our sinfulness and calls us to a larger loyalty. And this call, when we are willing to listen and respond to it, inevitably involves our whole lives. Something of this order is what occurs in the real worship of God; and it happens not only to his saints but also to the common ordinary run of sinners, to us.

"Conscience" is a slippery term for philosophical or theological discussion; but in common parlance we are perhaps clearer as to its meaning. The word refers not alone to our consciousness that the sin in our lives is displeasing to God, but further, to the sense of obligation to confess what is wrong and embrace what is right. Thus Hamlet was partly correct: "conscience doth make cowards of us all" when we are considering murder or suicide. But Hamlet's famous line is no sound analysis of other problems of living; conscience often makes just the opposite of cowards. Conscience drives us from the sanctuary into the market place, and impels some of us to enunciate the ideals of the sanctuary as opposed to the market place. Those who are so impelled believe that they are still worshiping God, and that not to speak out would be a denial of their own experience of worship. When we inquire as to the extent to which any society allows freedom of worship, then we are inevitably pushed to the query as to whether that society permits, or ought to permit, actions that flow from that worship because they are conceived to be absolute demands imposed by God on the worshiper. Our two questions in this area are: First, what do we as Christians believe that our faith demands? In the light of the Christian ethic, what is the desirable degree of freedom for the exercise of conscience? Second, what do we as citizens possess? In the light of the American development, what is the actual extent to which our government permits this exercise of conscience?

God Must Be Supreme

As to the first question, the Christian ethic as I understand it covets that form of political order in which the state recognizes the duty of each citizen to follow the leadings of his own conscience, when that conscience is based on religious faith; and to do so not merely in restricted matters of religious worship, narrowly defined, but in any area in which his conscience speaks to him. The record of Christians in support of such a thesis is not good, for here, even as in freedom of worship, the church as well as the state has often winced at, even betrayed, such a position through the centuries.[1]

Yet the stand of Jesus seems to be clear, if we are willing to trace patiently the implications of the remarks and actions that are attributed to him. Moreover, we find once again that Jesus is debtor in his point of view to the prophetic line of thought in Israel; and we should not use the term "Christian ethic" so as to exclude those Jews who fully subscribe to its conclusions. Like Moses on the Mount, like Samuel before Agag, like Amos, Hosea, and Micah, Jesus' ethical demands are absolute in the allegiance they call for. There is no justification in his thought for the moral holiday, or for setting up certain categories of living in which the ethic is understood as inapplicable. Nowhere do we find him diluting the moral demand: "Thou shalt love the Lord when it is expedient to do so; thou shalt love thy neighbor on Monday, Wednesday, and Friday."

Nor was it his example. After the baptism he wrestled with his conscience in the wilderness, and refused to be tempted to other than what he understood to be God's way. At Caesarea Philippi he could have compromised, but did not. In Gethsemane he faced and resisted the one last chance to escape the voice of God to him.[2] Who follow in his train? Martyrs and saints and humble, nameless men who realize and freely succumb to the absoluteness of God's demands on their lives.

For the man of religious faith this voice of God must be answered whether or not the state recognizes that it must. Yet Jesus is not remembered as having attacked the state as such.[3] That is, he does not seem to have assumed that the state would always and automatically be in opposition to the individual's obedience of God. The way is open for the inference—nor does any contrary inference seem to make sense—that Jesus, if he had been faced with the question, would have believed it desirable that the state recognize that the individual's first duty is to obey God.

But it is only to us in modern times that no contrary inference seems to make sense. Let it be freely admitted that, given a different set of circumstances from our own, Christians through the centuries have concluded differently. When state and church have been united, often no need for such an inference has been felt. When state and church have been poles apart, often no danger to Christian conscience has been recognized. In his day Paul could write to the Romans: "Let every person be subject to the governing authorities. For there is no authority except from God, and those that exist have been instituted by God."[4]

But times changed, and governmental authorities began to be suspicious that Christians could not become good citizens. Thus Christians themselves, faced with an unfriendly state, came to different conclusions, sometimes swinging to the opposite extreme of seeing the state as the work of Satan. All through these shifts of interpretation, however, the basic principle remained the same: man's first duty is to love and obey God. In such a situation as ours, where the state is neither antithetical to nor identical with the church, the reasonable inference from the principle on the one hand, and on the other the fact that Jesus did not condemn government per se, seems to be that the state itself should give recognition to the sovereignty of God over man's conscience.

Let us look, then, to our own day. Take, for example, the particular problem of our testimony on the individual's participation in war. We are aware that the pacifist declares that he is following the voice of God as he hears it. Certainly we need to be equally aware that the nonpacifist is doing likewise, though he comes out of his soul searching with a different personal strategy. There is no particular problem here in our attitude toward the pacifist, for we all agree that the pacifist may not base his testimony on fear, or desire to escape, but must be in truth a conscientious objector to the war system. The same is true for the Christian nonpacifist: he cannot justify his participation in war on the grounds that the state has decided the matter for him. That the state says so is never enough for the Christian; the individual conscience must also say so.[5] Here we come to the application of this illustration to our concern: the Christian ethic as presently understood can look with full favor on a political form of organization only

when and if that government officially recognizes the duty
the citizen has to his own conscience, in all areas of social
living, as being superior to his duty to take into account the
will of the state.[6]

The Negative Recognition

The second question must now be faced: How far can a
man in our society exercise his conscience? The answer may
be a surprise: We in America come remarkably close to
possessing the recognition on the part of the state of the rights
and demands of conscience. Our brief excursion into colonial
days, in the preceding chapter, is sufficient to convince us that
this recognition was not present among us then. Moreover,
since this aspect of religious freedom is in a sense an extension
of freedom to worship, we should not have expected it to
develop until after freedom to worship had itself been fully
secured. But when that freedom was gained, first by Virginia
and later by other states and the Federal Government, then
we should expect it to be tested in the give and take of civil
life.

Now normal behavior is not going to test it; it is only the
unusual idea or action that can serve as a real challenge, the
idea or action that is out of line with the prevailing thought or
practice of the community. How far shall we put up with
irregularity? What kind of irregularity shall we put up with?
Our belief in freedom has been tested by all sorts of heterodoxy
through the years of our national life. If the supremacy of
conscience is truly recognized by a government, we should
expect to find that two conditions are being met. First, when
the irregularity is not allowed, and yet when no "clear and

present danger" to the integrity of the state is involved, we should expect the state to base its prohibition on grounds of conscience, the conscience of the majority of the citizens. Second, when the irregularity is allowed, we should expect the state to base its permission again on the grounds of conscience, this time the conscience of the individual concerned.

This is close to what we do find in the legal decisions. First, we shall explore the situation in which the irregularity was not allowed. Among the various aberrations that might be examined, polygamy serves as an especially illuminating illustration. The Church of Jesus Christ of Latter-Day Saints believed, among other things, that a man should be allowed to have more than one wife. Popular books and movies have dramatized their struggle to find a land in which they could practice their beliefs, a struggle that took them from New York to Missouri and Illinois and then on to Utah, in their thrilling migration in the middle of the last century.

But even Utah was not Utopia for them. Soon after the Mormons arrived there, the United States acquired the area from Mexico; and American citizens frowned on polygamy which, incidentally, seems never to have been practiced by more than a few of the faithful. Beginning in 1850, when Utah was admitted into the United States as a territory, a titanic conflict developed between the Mormons and the Federal Government. Statutes forbidding the practice were passed, but the Mormons continually found ways to get around them.[7]

It was not until 1878 that the Supreme Court had its first opportunity to give an opinion on the legality of the polygamy laws. In this case, *Reynolds v. United States*, the statutes were upheld. The Mormons had entered the plea that, since the practice was part of their faith, their religious freedom had been denied. The decision of the Court, however, was that "a party's religious belief cannot be accepted as a justification for his committing an overt act, made criminal by the law of the land."[8]

But why was polygamy "made criminal by the law of the land"? Further incidents in the struggle with the Mormons gave the Supreme Court a chance to elaborate on this judgment. In 1882 an act was passed prohibiting polygamists from voting. Once again the Mormons appealed on the grounds that their religious liberty had been violated. Nevertheless, in *Davis v. Beason*, 1890, the Court upheld the act, and stated: "Bigamy and polygamy are crimes by the laws of all civilized and Christian countries. . . . To extend exemption from punishment for such crimes would be to shock the moral judgment of the community."[9]

This "moral judgment of the community" was made more explicit by a third important case. In 1887 Congress repealed the incorporation of the Mormon Church, and this act was upheld by the Supreme Court in 1890 on the grounds that the Church was an organized rebellion. In this case, *Late Corporation of the Church of Jesus Christ of Latter-Day Saints v. United States*, Justice Bradley said:

The organization of a community for the spread and practice of polygamy is, in a measure, a return to barbarism. It is contrary to the spirit of Christianity and of the civilization which Christianity has produced in the Western World. The question, therefore, is whether the promotion of such a nefarious system and practice, so repugnant to our laws and to the principles of our civilization, is to be allowed to continue by the sanction of the government itself. . . . The State has a perfect right to prohibit polygamy, and all other open offences against the enlightened sentiment of man-kind, notwithstanding the pretence of religious conviction by which they may be advocated and practiced.[10]

Christian Morality and the Law

Thus the struggle with the Mormons came to an end. But it is interesting to note that the fight was won by the Federal Government only by its recognition of its connection with Christianity and by its reference to Christian morality as part of the law of the land. Such a relationship had been affirmed much earlier, the first notable statement being by Chancellor Kent, of the New York State Supreme Court, in 1811. In the now famous action *People v. Ruggles* it was held that

Christianity being recognized by the law, therefore blasphemy against God, and profane ridicule of Christ or the Holy Scripture, are punishable at common law.[11]

Kent elaborated:

The people of this state, in common with the people of this country, profess the general doctrines of Christianity, as the rule of their faith and practice; and to scandalize the author of these doctrines is not only, in a religious point of view extremely impious, but even in respect to the obligations due to society, is a gross violation of decency and good order.[12]

This case, Kent continued,

assumes that we are a Christian people, and the morality of the country is deeply ingrafted upon Christianity.[13]

He pointed out that the Constitution of New York discarded religious establishments, but

this declaration . . . never meant to withdraw religion in general, and with it the best sanctions of moral and social obligation from all consideration and notice of the law.[14]

Chancellor Kent's judgment that Christian morality is part of the law of the land has been followed throughout the nation. As far as I can discover, in no court, state or Federal, has this case been specifically disapproved, while countless courts have cited his opinion as authority in similar cases.[15]

But it is important to recognize that it is only Christian morality, not the Christian religion as a whole, that has in some sense come to be part of the common law. This conclusion is verified and Kent's position is illuminated by a leading Pennsylvania case of 1824, *Updegraph v. Commonwealth*, that also deals with blasphemy. Justice Duncan, delivering the opinion that "maliciously to vilify the Christian religion is an indictable offence," pointed out:

Christianity, general Christianity, is, and always has been, a part of the common law of Pennsylvania; . . . not Christianity founded on any particular religious tenets; not Christianity with an established church and tithes and spiritual courts; but Christianity with the liberty of conscience to all men.[16]

Then followed the statement in which he indicated that by Christianity he meant specifically Christian morality:

Christianity is part of the common law of this state. It is not proclaimed by the commanding voice of any human superior, but expressed in the calm and mild accents of customary law. Its foundations are broad, and strong, and deep; they are laid in the authority, the interest, the affections of the people. Waiving all questions of hereafter, it is the purest system of morality, the firmest auxiliary, and the only stable support of all human laws.[17]

These two old decisions are cited because they established the precedents that are still being followed today, when the unusual details of a legal action call for it.[18] But we must be careful to understand exactly what it is that these cases, and many others like them, including the ones on polygamy, really represent. The contention is not that the courts have invaded the religious or spiritual realm, and sought to pass out judgments on spiritual offenses. This has not happened, and certainly ought not to happen. The law sees blasphemy, for example, as a temporal offense, a breach of the peace. What the law understands as Christian morality enters its decisions only so far as to serve as an explanation of this breach, because the law may not allow the moral precepts and religious faith of a majority of the citizens to be vilified. The law notes that a majority of the citizens are Christians, or at least nominal followers of what it takes to be Christian morality; and its appropriation of Christian ethics as part of the common law is dependent on this fact, not on some inherent virtue that the law sees in that system of morality.[19] If Christian morality should ever cease to be the ethical code of the majority, then the law would no longer be forced to take it into account.[20]

Perhaps a parenthesis should be inserted here to the effect that we are dealing of course not with the Christian ethic itself so much as with certain moral conclusions at which Christians and others have arrived. The law calls a particular ethic Christian, rather than trying to understand and apply the real Christian ethic. Yet no more should be expected because of the nature of the Christian ethic itself, which in essence is not a legalism at all. It is a matter of the relationship between God and man, and thus between man and his neighbor, a relationship which, for man, is dependent on his faith, his acceptance of it, rather than on his good works, his obedience to law.[21] Yet his true acceptance of the relationship that God freely offers him will involve him in good works; and a conscientious exploration of what good works consists in will usually lead him to adopt what is commonly thought of as moral behavior and to forego immorality as it is customarily defined. These moral conclusions of the Christian inevitably become accepted in the popular mind as Christian ethics; this is the Christian morality of which the law takes cognizance.

Nevertheless, even with these necessary refinements, the law's recognition goes further than merely noting that the majority of the citizens are attached to something it calls Christian morality. Involved also is a recognition of what this means, what the Christian conscience has to say with respect to certain practices that may arise. Let us go back to the subject of polygamy: there the state clearly enunciates the Christian view of the matter. The "moral judgment of the community" that it upholds is not secular but religious, specifically termed "Christian," though it might have been with more accuracy called "Hebrew-Christian." The judgments against the Mormons were not, as they declared, the denial of all religious liberty and the annulment of conscience, for there were two liberties and two consciences at issue. One was the Mormons'; the other was the group conscience of the people of the United States, a conscience defined by presumably Christian standards. These decisions, therefore, were an assertion of Christian conscience, so as to root out what the people felt to be an unchristian practice. So distressed and determined was the Federal Government, pressed by the sense of the outrage of its citizens, that when Utah was admitted to statehood in 1896, Congress required that polygamy be prohibited by the State Constitution, and further, that that article, Article III, was not to be amended "without the consent of

the United States."[22] This was literally making assurance
doubly sure.

The conclusion of this matter is that any practice that out-
rages the Christian conscience of the citizens will not be allowed. Thus conscience is legally recognized as a negative
element in the ordering of American society, and its supremacy
is asserted in the justifying of prohibitive measures.

But this is the easier side of the question. The mass can
stand on conscience against the individual or the small group,
but can the individual ever stand on conscience against the
mass? Is there a positive as well as a negative recognition by
official organs of government of the supremacy of conscience?
Is the Government's attitude toward an unpopular act of conscience ever permissive instead of prohibitive? This is the more
difficult problem, perhaps the most difficult that any state,
saddled with the responsbility of keeping order, can face.

The Positive Recognition

As bearing on such questions the famous Macintosh case will
come immediately to mind. Professor Douglas Clyde Macintosh of Yale University, a Canadian by nationality, applied
for naturalization in 1925, and according to the questionnaire
then in use, was asked to answer the question, "Are you willing
to bear arms in defense of the United States?" Though not a
pacifist—he had actually taken part in World War I—he refused
to reply in the unequivocal affirmative. On religious grounds
he reserved the right of decision as to whether or not he would
fight in some future war. The question and answer were
hypothetical for him, for he was then over the age for active
combatants. Nevertheless his application was denied, and the

matter climbed through the courts, with varying decisions, until in 1931 it reached the Supreme Court.[23] By a vote of five to four the Supreme Court confirmed the original denial of his application, a decision that was in line with *United States v. Schwimmer*, of 1929, in which a Hungarian woman was not admitted to citizenship because of her pacifist position.[24]

Writing the majority opinion, Justice Sutherland said:

We are a Christian people, according to one another the equal right of religious freedom, and acknowledging with reverence the duty of obedience to the will of God. But, also, we are a nation with the duty to survive; a nation whose constitution contemplates war as well as peace; whose government must go forward upon the assumption, and safely can proceed upon no other, that unqualified allegiance to the nation and submission and obedience to the laws of the land, as well those made for war as those made for peace, is not inconsistent with the will of God.[25]

In other words, the nation's will must be interpreted as the will of God. If any citizens feel the two to be separable, and choose to be loyal to God's will, they are out of bounds. Their only course of action must be "unqualified allegiance," "submission," and "obedience." If conscience should dictate an action contrary to the will of the state, then in that case there would be no such thing as freedom of conscience. There is no duty to a moral power higher than the state, for the simple reason that there is no moral power higher than the state. "Unqualified allegiance to the nation . . . is not inconsistent with the will of God," and therefore the will of God is not something higher than the nation's will or the nation's interpretation of God's will. Thus ran the reasoning of the majority of the Court.

So far, so bad. If this were where we had to stop, we should be forced to conclude that the desirable recognition of the freedom of conscience and the actual situation in the United States were two different things and pretty far apart. But that is not the end of the story. One of the sequels was the upheaval among churchmen. Repeated efforts to persuade Congress to pass legislation nullifying the decision were unsuccessful, and the clamor of religious leaders was of no avail.[26]

But another sequel, with a different outcome, was the case of James Louis Girouard, which came before the Supreme Court in 1946. Girouard, another Canadian, applied for citizenship, but refused to agree to "take up arms in defense of this country," though he was willing to serve in the Army in some noncombatant capacity. As a member of the Seventh Day Adventists he said, "It is purely a religious matter with me. I have no political or personal reasons other than that."[27] By a vote of five to three, with one abstention, the Court decided that Girouard's conscientious objection should not exclude him from citizenship. In so doing the Court explicitly overruled the Schwimmer and Macintosh cases, and *United States v. Bland*,[28] a similar action.

In the majority opinion Justice Douglas faced the central issue squarely. With hearty approval he referred to the position of the four dissenters in the Macintosh case. These four, Chief Justice Hughes and Justices Holmes, Brandeis, and Stone, were perhaps the most distinguished members of the Court at that time, and those who deplored the Macintosh decision took what comfort they could from the weight and prestige of the dissenting judges, and from the grounds of the dissent as phrased in the opinion of the Chief Justice. Hughes had written:

When one's belief collides with the power of the state, the latter is supreme within its sphere and submission or punishment follows. But in the forum of conscience, duty to a moral power higher than the state has always been maintained. . . . The essence of religion is belief in a relation to God involving duties superior to those arising from any human relation. . . . One cannot speak of religious liberty, with proper appreciation of its essential and historic significance, without assuming the existence of a belief in supreme allegiance to the will of God.[29]

These lofty sentiments did not prevail in 1931, but now at last, in 1946, the Court itself was recognizing that Hughes' position was more cogent than that of Sutherland. Justice Douglas argued:

Refusal to bear arms is not necessarily a sign of disloyalty or a lack of attachment to our institutions. One may serve his country faithfully and devotedly, though his religious scruples make it impossible for him to shoulder a rifle. Devotion to one's country can be as real and as enduring among noncombatants as among combatants. One may adhere to what he deems to be his obligation to God and yet assume all military risks to ensure victory. The effort of war is indivisible; and those whose religious scruples prevent them from killing are no less patriots than those whose special traits or handicaps result in their assignment to duties far behind the fighting front. Each is making the utmost contribution according to his capacity.[30]

And what defines "capacity" in the eyes of the law for the sincere noncombatant? It is religious conscience. Douglas continued:

The struggle for religious liberty has through the centuries been an effort to accommodate the demands of the State to the conscience of the individual. The victory for freedom of thought recorded in our Bill of Rights recognizes that in the domain of conscience there is a moral power higher than the State. Throughout the ages men have suffered death rather than subordinate their allegiance to God to the authority of the State. Freedom of religion guaranteed by the First Amendment is the product of that struggle.[31]

An interesting footnote to the decision is that among the minority of three was Chief Justice Stone, one of the famous four dissenters in the Macintosh case fifteen years before. Writing the minority opinion, Stone maintained that he himself had not changed his point of view but that Congress, by its inaction through the years, had confirmed the Court's earlier construction. Thus he did not feel it proper to overrule the former decision, even though he did not agree with it. But Douglas had an answer for his opinion:

It is at best treacherous to find in Congressional silence alone the adoption of a controlling rule of law. We do not think under the circumstances of this legislative history that we can properly place on the shoulders of Congress the burden of the Court's own error.[32]

The Extent and Limits of Conscience

The Court made an error, and then the Court reversed itself. The Court proscribed conscience, and then the Court removed the proscription. This was great good news to lovers of liberty, and most of all to those whose love of liberty was rooted in their religious faith. But we pause to note one curious fact: the Girouard case received nothing like as much attention as the Macintosh case from churchmen, scholars, and the general public, and certainly nothing like as much as it deserved. It is almost as if we should rather scream at the defeats suffered by liberty than rejoice at the victories won in its name. Perhaps we should; and perhaps there is something healthy in such a reaction. For if "eternal vigilance" is the proverbial price, surely it is safer for that vigilance to be exercised on behalf of the threats to liberty than on behalf of its extensions.

Yet this hardly explains the treatment accorded these two cases in recent scholarly literature. The two monumental works in this field in recent days are M. Searle Bates's *Religious Liberty: An Inquiry* and Anson Phelps Stokes's *Church and State in the United States*. As to the first, Bates could not have referred to Girouard because his work was published in 1945, the year before the decision; but it is surprising to discover that only once in his 600 pages, and that in a brief footnote, does he mention the Macintosh case with its distressing overtones as to the limits of religious liberty in this country.[33]

Stokes's treatment is even more inexplicable, for his massive three-volume work of over 2,700 pages was not published until 1950, and yet nowhere does he refer to the Girouard decision. He discusses both the Schwimmer and the Macintosh cases, calls attention to the brave dissenting opinions in each action, and notes that churchmen were upset over the outcome; and thus he seems to have been fully aware of their negative significance for one of his general theses, that in America we have achieved a remarkable degree of religious liberty.[34] But he fails to note that case that, reversing both the Schwimmer and the Macintosh decisions, most clearly supports his own position.

Some measure of justification for these omissions may be found in the fact that both authors deal with the problem of the Jehovah's Witnesses, and the outcome of that strange sect's legal difficulties was interpreted as a great victory for freedom of conscience.[35] This victory was achieved in 1943, three years before the Girouard decision. A brief review may be useful both to note the importance of the actions involved, and yet to throw further light on the decisiveness of the Girouard judgment.

The issue of the Jehovah's Witnesses came to attention in 1938, when the Gobitis children of Minersville, Pennsylvania, were excluded from school because of their refusal to comply with a school order that required them to salute the flag. This was a gesture that the Jehovah's Witnesses felt was idolatrous, compromising their supreme allegiance to God. The first trial of such matters before the Supreme Court was in 1940, when by a vote of eight to one the Court ruled against the Gobitis children.[36] But Justice Stone, who had stood with Hughes and the others in the Macintosh case, was again the dissenter, and thus the protagonist of religious freedom. He said:

> Government has a right to survive, and powers conferred upon it are not necessarily set at naught by the express prohibitions of the Bill of Rights. . . . It may suppress religious practices dangerous to morals, and presumably those also which are inimical to public safety, health and good order. . . . But it is a long step, and one which I am unable to take, to the position that government may, as a supposed educational measure and as a means of disciplining the young, compel public affirmations which violate their religious conscience.[37]

Only three years later the Court had so completely reversed itself as to make Stone's lone dissent the majority opinion. The matter rose again because the effect of the 1940 decision was to make the Jehovah's Witnesses, who would not give ground on the issue of flag saluting, subject to prosecution for not sending their children to school, in a situation in which the children were expelled from school because they would not salute. This awkward business was resolved when the Court voted by six to three to overturn the previous judgment. In the majority opinion Justice Jackson said,

To sustain the compulsory flag salute we are required to say that a Bill of Rights which guards the individual's right to speak his own mind left open to public authorities to compel him to utter what is not in his mind.[38]

The reversal was hailed as a triumph for freedom, and indeed it was. A great and powerful nation had lent the protection of its courts to what many people felt was a disreputable sect, and had cited the nation's belief in religious freedom as its cause for so doing. And yet the decision was not as significant for the issue now under discussion as was the Girouard case three years later. This is true for two reasons. First, the absurdity in which the school boards and courts had become involved, and the relative unimportance of both the group and the act in question, had become abundantly and embarrassingly clear, and these considerations were attested to in Justice Jackson's opinion.[39] But in the Girouard case the Court was fully aware of the significance of its decision as involving something much more important than a musical comedy situation, and in neither majority nor minority opinions was there any hint that the Court thought the matter was unimportant. Second, and more pertinent, the Court was aware that the whole Gobitis sequence ending in 1943 did not erase from the books the decision in the Macintosh case; and until that decision was reversed, a crucial recognition of the rights of conscience was missing. By the Court's express statement, the Macintosh decision was not overruled in 1943, but in 1946;[40] and thus it is the Girouard case that stands as the most far-reaching decision of the Supreme Court in the matter of freedom of conscience.

And this is what the Girouard case means: even in such a vital matter as bearing arms in the country's behalf, when its whole integrity as a nation is being threatened, a man may successfully plead conscience in his defense of personal actions that are contrary to the will of the state. Yet lest we seem to conclude that this freedom of conscience is unlimited, it behooves us to notice some of its necessary boundaries. First of all, this is the freedom of a Christian conscience, a conscience shaped by the moral precepts of the Hebrew-Christian tradition. It is not freedom for whim. To persuade our courts to uphold his liberty in this regard a man must be able to show that the Hebrew-Christian ethic has some understanding, if not unanimous endorsement, of his point of view. The Mormons failed because they could not successfully link their advocacy of polygamy to Christian concepts, for the Christian sanction was on the other side; Girouard succeeded because he could, even though others disagree with him as to what the Christian ethic calls for in the matter of bearing arms.

Secondly, it is the state and not the church that makes—and inescapably must make, in our form of relationship between the two—the judgment as to whether the attribution of one's act to the Christian ethic is valid and sincere. Thus the extent to which freedom of conscience is recognizable by the state depends on that state's—that is, the law's—understanding of the Christian ethic. If the law does not understand the Christian ethic in sufficiently broad terms, churchmen may cry to high heaven to no immediate avail, as they did in both the Macintosh and the Gobitis cases. Part of the proper protection of the freedom of conscience, therefore, is the effort continually to interpret the demands of the Christian ethic, so that the author-

itative organs of our governmental life may base their allowance
of liberty on as sound an understanding as possible. Who
knows? Perhaps the protests of churchmen did play some important part in the subsequent reversal of those two decisions.

The third limitation is related to the second. The state must
make its decisions on the basis of a careful balancing between
the rival claims of freedom and order. As we noticed in Chapter I, freedom is not antithetical to order; in essence it both
presupposes and subsumes it. Yet for any one individual claim-
ing Christian conscience as his guide, a tension between the
two may often develop. If he presses his claim before governmental authority, he transfers his tension to the state. In such
a situation the state cannot escape its twofold obligation, to
maintain both freedom and order. The state's formula for doing
this is reflected in many of the quotations above: the state is
obliged to support freedom up to the point where—Madison's
phrasing—"under color of religion the preservation of equal
liberty and the existence of the State are manifestly endan-
gered." In other words, the right of conscience does not carry
with it the right to escape the penalty for violating the law.[41]
The recognition of conscience does not call for the abdication
by the state from its duty to maintain itself, especially in times
of national emergency.[42]

Such a formula of course is not precise, and mistakes are
often made. But the surprise unfolded by our national story
is not that we have sometimes allowed this obligation to justify
our restrictions of liberty, but rather that we have allowed
liberty to grow and flourish in spite of it. Let it be recognized
that in the hands of individual courts and judges our practice
often falls short of our theory; but the remarkable fact is that

our political theory now recognizes, and even our practice often permits, the individual citizen to defend himself successfully on the grounds of conscience, even when that conscience is in conflict with the state. Freedom is not license, and limitations of the sorts just described are present; but freedom in America is, among other things, freedom of conscience. It is the recognition of the supremacy of conscience. This is a great and rare possession. It comes as close as such a diverse human society as ours is ever likely to come, to maintaining the Christian principle that God's demands are prior demands, and to acknowledging the Christian desire that the state subscribe to that recognition.

CHAPTER IV

The Independence
of Church and State

"Separation" is Bewildering

THE religious liberty of an individual is defined not alone by the freedom to worship which he is allowed and by the extent to which the rights of his conscience are recognized. It turns also on his society's approval or disapproval of his associations, the latitude he possesses in joining with others of like mind; and thus the freedom of such groups, or organizations, or churches, both to be independent of the direction of civil authority and to participate in civil affairs. The third aspect of religious liberty, therefore, has to do with the relationships between church and state.

Such questions as the following call for our attention: Does the state show favoritism to one or another ecclesiastical body, or does it turn to all an impartial face? If the latter, is its impartiality friendly to all organized religion, or merely neutral? Does it prohibit, or condone, or actually invite, the participation of churches in civil affairs? And once again, we shall divide our discussion into the two questions, What is desirable in this matter from the point of view of Christian ethics? and, What is the actual situation in the United States?

But before we proceed to this task, we must pause to point out a special difficulty that is involved. In Chapter I it was noted that today we in America are confused as to the meaning of liberty. We need to realize now that confusion is especially prevalent as to the relationship of ecclesiastical and governmental organizations. It springs from our use of the pat phrase, "the separation of church and state." Here it is supposed is the great key to the proper answering of all our questions. Educators pontificate, churchmen dogmatize, and politicians invoke its sanctions in the mellifluous rhythm of its syllables. "Separation" is allowed to sum up both the actual and the desirable relationship of the two entities.

But it won't do. As a phrase it says both too little and too much, and it means too many different things to too many people. For example, take the Catholics and their use of it. Some Catholics say that separation is what we have and ought to have; others, that it is what we have but ought not to have; and still others, that it is what we do not have and ought not to have.[1] So far as I am aware, no Catholic has gone so far as to say that separation is what we do not have but ought to have! The variety of interpretations among Catholics is not likely to include this position.

Yet Catholics are not in as great disagreement as to the proper relationship between church and state, or even as to the actual situation, as this variety might indicate. The differences are caused only in part by the divergences of opinion among them;[2] in greater part they stem from the wide variety of interpretations among them on the meaning of the phrase.

Similarly, Protestants who want substantially the same relationship between church and state divide into two groups, one desiring and the other deploring what they call "separation." Protestants who agree substantially as to the nature of the relationship that now exists also divide into two groups, one thinking of it as "separation," and the other as a contradiction of "separation." Non-Christians of many stripes fall into the same pattern. Again, the divisions are caused in great measure by differences in their interpretation of the meaning of the phrase. Such is the confusion among us when these people agree in the main in their desire or their analysis. But certainly they do not always agree; and when they disagree, confusion is worse confounded.[3]

But even if the phrase were not misunderstood and misused it would still be inadequate to describe fairly either the actual or the desirable relationship between church and state. First of all, the phrase is inadequate to sum up the actuality, either at the time when the principle was promulgated or for the present scene. In the first instance the phrase seems to have been Jefferson's. He spoke of a "wall of separation"[4] that should exist, but as we shall see the term "wall" was an exaggeration designed to emphasize the difference between the system of the past and the relationship he desired. The principle for which he fought never did call, nor does it call now, for the construction of a "wall" between church and state. As the records of the time amply testify, absolute cleavage between the two was neither the intention nor the creation of Jefferson and the other founding fathers.[5]

Thus, to say—as many now do—that complete separation is not possible is to beg at least part of the question. Let us grant that it is not possible. But possible or no, if the case were that it was the historic ideal, then to the extent to which we sought to base present policy on historical antecedents, to that extent we should have to deal with it, and in one way or another make our peace with its impossibility. This is in fact the strategy of many who so misread history.

The misinterpretation is particularly unfortunate for those who believe that church and state should co-ordinate their efforts in at least some areas of social activity, for they find themselves in the position of confessing that, however much logic may be on their side, history is against them. Not being able to change what they take to be history, they must attempt the more difficult task of seeking to redefine, supposedly without historical support, what the relationship of church and state should be.[6] But history is on their side; and by ignorance of that fact they weaken their case considerably at the bar of public opinion.

This same misunderstanding strengthens unjustifiably the position of those today who want state and church to occupy separate, watertight compartments. They look around them and note what is of course the fact of the present situation, namely, that much mutual recognition and co-operation exist. Then they call on their misunderstanding of history to buttress their bewailing the modern scene.[7] They have full right, of course, to state their position and seek to persuade others of it. But history, rightly conceived, puts an obstacle, not the seal of triumph, on their argument. The present actuality, as these folks recognize, and the historical intention, which they do not understand, alike substantiate the thesis that complete separation is an inaccurate rendering of the American way of dealing with church-state relationships.

Let it be noted that the distinction being pursued is not between separation on the one hand and organic connection on the other; rather, the distinction is between complete separation, a "wall," on the one hand, and on the other a measure of separateness, involving among other things an organic disconnection. It is absolute separation that neither history nor present practice supports; but some kind or degree of separation is supported by history and honored in present practice.

Yet that very phrase, "some kind or degree of separation," gives us a clue to the resolution of the difficulty, for it is a contradiction in terms. "Separation" is the wrong word, not only historically and for the present time, but linguistically, and thus we should find some other way of summarizing our analysis of things as they have been and are. The relationship between church and state is exceedingly complex, and has many varied aspects. The need therefore is for some term that does not refer, or call to mind, only the one aspect of standoffishness.[8]

Moreover, "separation of church and state" is an inadequate phrase to sum up the desideratum. As a word, "separation" is bound to sound strange to Christians, or even to non-Christians who are firmly committed to democracy. On one level the democratic faith, and on a deeper level the Christian faith, call for the recognition of the relatedness of all men one to another. The terms used to summarize their desires in any area of activity dare not contradict this basic element in their faith.

For "separation" is a loaded word. The nature of the inferences it provokes in Christian and democratic minds is such as to prejudice convinced Christians and democrats against a full and free consideration of the issues revolving around it. "Separation of church and state" implies no contact between the two, and runs the risk of implying no application of the ideals of each on the other. This goes against the Christian, democratic grain. Once again, the phrase serves us ill.

The Christian Ideal

The problem is not solved by finding or coining a new word to take the place of the old; resolution will come only through analysis, a dispassionate examination of the relationship between church and state, without dependence on "separation" or any other one phrase to sum up the total situation and point of view. Such an examination must hold in juxtaposition both the desirable and the actual, both the Christian goal and the American development. From this otherwise negative beginning we can salvage one positive realization, and in the process reiterate one contention on which this volume is based, namely, that the relationship the Christian ethic covets is in close and surprising parallel the kind that exists in the United States today and whose existence is supported by our national history. The only thing wrong with our speaking of the actual and the desirable in one breath is the phrase we choose to use our breath on. Let us have done, then, with "separation of church and state," and proceed to our task.

But in this complex subject we strive to escape one difficulty only to fall into another. Christian thinking on the relationship of church and state is even more diverse than on other aspects of religious liberty. The practice of Christians around the world is even less enlightening.[9] The inferences we draw from Biblical thought, particularly from Jesus, are tenuous and debatable. In the conclusions to which we shall arrive we must take special pains to escape provincialism of point of view, the partial vision of both the Protestant and the American.

Yet we begin boldly by noting that the incident in Jesus'

life most commonly taken as instructive in this matter is easily misunderstood. "Render therefore to Caesar the things that are Caesar's and to God the things that are God's" has nothing determinative to do with our subject. This is the proof-text method of reading the Scriptures, and such a method we have eschewed. Some folks employ the quotation as decisive proof that Jesus believed in complete disconnection between church and state.[10] A few try to interpret it in the other direction, that since in Jesus' view everything belonged to God, he was in this incident setting up a hierarchy of interests, not two separate spheres; that Caesar and God could be served at the same time, for Caesar's interests were encompassed in God's.[11]

But the episode will not bear the weight of such interpretations, for at least two reasons. The first is that, even if Jesus had had in mind the relation of synagogue and empire—a shaky assumption—the modern political situation is so altogether different from that of the first century as to require of us some other approach to the problem. Second, Jesus was simply answering a trick question in such a way as to escape the trap being laid for him. There is nothing in the Gospel record to suggest that he and his companions were aware that he was setting forth, or intending to set forth, a principle for the ordering of church-state relations for every society.[12]

This is not to say, however, that the incident can be dismissed as having no guidance to offer. First of all, the church has used it, for good or ill, and its use has itself shaped the thinking of the church, particularly in the first of the two directions just mentioned. More important, the saying bears the weight of at least negative inference, in the fashion of the over-all approach to Scripture that we are here trying to make. We are seeking to understand the atmosphere and trend of Biblical thought, rather than to make sweeping conclusions from one or another literal word; and the incident serves at least so far as not to contradict two general premises in which, we notice, the early church put reliance. The first of these, rooted in Old Testament thought, is that it was God, not man, that called the state into being; and since the episode does not picture Jesus as condemning the state, it fails to shake one's confidence that this principle is pertinent to the problem. The second premise has to do with the Great Command as the ruling guide of life; and whatever else the "Render . . ." passage means, it does not seem to counsel any dilution of the impact of that "law" on human affairs. For positive guidance, therefore, the incident leaves us free to search elsewhere in the Scriptures.

More suggestive and less treacherous for our concern is the grain-picking episode. Here Jesus did seem to defend the charge against him, this time that of breaking the Sabbath Law, not alone by linguistic rebuttal—David did it, why shouldn't we?— but also by conscious resort to the principle involved. "The Sabbath was made for man, not man for the Sabbath."[13] We can imagine that if the challenge had arisen in some other context Jesus would have been as quick to point out that any other institution or custom, originally designed for man's benefit, may become so legalized and rigid as to work to man's detriment. The state was made for man, not man for the state; the church was made for man, not man for the church.

Jesus did not assert that the insight was new with him. Here again he was playing the role of successor to the prophets rather than the priests.[14] For Judaism as well as Christianity has nurtured the strain of thought that, though it does not attack institutions as such, does condemn what has been called institutionalism. Not this incident alone but everything in Jesus' thinking upholds man as the important element—his welfare, his growth, his personal relationship with his Father. Nothing in Jesus' thought condones institutionalism. Moreover, the fact that the Great Command suffuses all his thinking can here be a positive as well as a negative aid to our understanding. Love of God and neighbor takes precedence over attachment to Sabbath Law or to any other effort to codify behavior and organize human relationships, if they should come in conflict with each other. Institutionalism is proscribed by the Great Command.

Let us not conclude too hastily that hence Jesus would have believed in the absence of an organic tie between church and state. On the contrary, he was a good enough Jew to think of the two as somehow belonging together. The idea of a theocracy was the Hebrew contribution to the problem of human government.[15] But the thought that the early church remembered that Jesus did express—the danger of institutionalism—would seem to have required of him, if occasion had ever demanded it, a protest against the glorification and sanctification of a partnership between the two institutions as an end in itself. Occasion never called for such a protest from him; but the occasions have risen in limitless numbers within the bounds of Christendom since the time of Constantine to the present, that is, since church and state first joined hands. Church history, both Catholic and Protestant, shows the temptations and submissions to institutionalism when organic connection was present in any form.[16]

But though abuses were often deplored, and sometimes produced active rebellion, the Hebrew-Christian theocratic ideal was too firmly implanted to give way easily to some other concept. Moreover, until the formation of our Federal government, the conditions never seemed to be ripe for the creation of a more satisfactory arrangement. Up to that time the faith of the citizens of any one commonwealth was sufficiently homogeneous to appear to justify the consolidation of the institutions of that faith and that citizenship. God was the Lord of all life, which meant, of government; and Paul was often called to mind: "The powers that be are ordained of God." Paul and the Christian succession generally have believed that governments perform necessary functions; and this much at least may be implied in "Render to Caesar the things that are Caesar's." The state needs association with the church in order to guarantee that its powers shall be exercised in line with God's will. If the state abuses its God-given trust, this is cause for criticizing and correcting the abuse, not for overturning the theory. For the theory of church-state connection is good: it is only the practice that is sometimes bad. So ran the thinking of nearly all Christians, Catholic and Protestant, as long as most Christians of any one country were also of one church.[17]

But the circumstances in America in the latter half of the eighteenth century, which as we shall see produced a new arrangement, also produced a new theory, yet one that need not be taken as ideal, or even applicable, to all other countries. When there are a multitude of denominations, with none holding a dominant position, to pick out one for special governmental favors is to run an even graver risk of developing the spirit of institutionalism. All of them seek to speak God's will. The state is the civil authority for all of them. The state must own its subservience to God, and thus needs the counsel of all the churches, but of no one more than another. This calls for the equality of all religious sects in the eyes of the law, which implies both the absence of organic ties between state and any church, and the presence of support for religion—though not for sectarianism. Such now appears to be the Christian concept of the proper relationship for America, a safer guard against the offenses of either state or church than merely the right of protest and rebellion at the excesses of a church-state establishment.[18]

We recognize, of course, that organic connection may not always make for institutionalism. It is possible to conceive of some other society than our own in which a legal tie could exist without abrogating the principle of the primacy of man's needs over those of an institution, church or state, or of the two more fundamental principles of God's sovereignty and the Great Command. Some such instance may now be offered in the complicated situation in Britain; one is impressed by the fact that many English nonconformists do not want disestablishment now, though many Church of England leaders do.[19] Yet our situation in America has been and is radically different. Finding that no definitive word on the issue has been spoken, but guided by the major premises of the Bible and the early church, we have sought to make a responsible adjustment to our own society. At least for the American scene, the conclusion to which the Christian ethic has come, in the Protestant interpretation of the problem, is that neither church nor state should have vested interest in the other.

The Virginia Victory

It has already been indicated that we did not always believe this way. Most of colonial America was founded on the old theory that church and state should properly possess some organic connection; this was as true for those who came to these shores to escape the Church of England as for those who brought the Anglican establishment with them. Various colonists had various attitudes toward the state church back home, but almost none of them had any desire to forego the supposed benefit of an alliance between a purified church and a benevolent state. To the extent to which they came to this country for religious reasons, they intended to establish God's society; and God's society should be indivisible.

But the organic association of church and state is a matter of degree, rather than kind. There is identity one with the other, there is union of the two, and there are varied degrees of intimate relations short of unity but all depending on some legal connection or favoritism. The colonies differed in the nature of their connections, depending on the roots in the Old World from which they drew their ideas and practices. But in all of them, ranging from the clear-cut establishments in such colonies as Massachusetts and Virginia, to the least tangible ties then existent in Pennsylvania and Rhode Island, the arm of the state was available to wield its power for the benefit or protection of the major religious group. The partnership was tight here, or loose there, but in all thirteen colonies the state and the church were in some degree of partnership with each other.[20]

This does not mean that all the colonies had what could properly be called an established church. On the contrary, no such clear-cut situation existed anywhere, once the homogeneity of the original group had been diluted by further immigration. Scholars tend to speak of Massachusetts, Connecticut, and Virginia as the three colonies that had a state church,[21] but in one sense none of these ever achieved either the Calvinist or the Anglican ideal of a theocracy;[22] and in another light other colonies from time to time, or throughout their colonial history, had something close to what those three possessed. New Netherlands looked on the Dutch Reformed as the established church body, and much later the Anglican Church was nominally if not actually established in its successor colony, New York.[23] In spite of Calvert's great experiment of toleration in Maryland, later the Anglican Church was legally established there also.[24] New Hampshire had many of the marks of establishment characteristic of Massachusetts,[25] as did the Carolinas and Georgia of Virginia.[26]

New Jersey and Delaware had no established church, nor did those three champions of toleration, Pennsylvania and Rhode Island, and Maryland for much of its colonial history.[27] But in all these places, as with those with actual or merely nominal establishments, at least some among the following ways of lending state support to church bodies were customary: proscriptions of public worship against certain groups; compulsory taxes for the support of favored bodies; disabilities, growing out of membership in certain churches, for voting, or holding public office, or taking oaths.[28]

No suggestion is being made that we should take any credit from any of the colonies or their leaders who fought and made progress for the cause of religious liberty. As has already been noted, the colonial efforts toward the establishment of freedom of worship were great. Many of the leaders in that movement, particularly Roger Williams,[29] were instrumental in the allied area of eliminating church-state ties. Many of the aforementioned influences for freedom of worship as distinct from toleration worked also toward this end. But after we give full credit, the fact is that full success in this regard was not achieved prior to the Revolutionary War.

Again, it was Virginia that led the way in legal action. The 1776 Bill of Rights did not disestablish the Church of England,[30] though it did embark the state on a course of action that necessarily led to disestablishment. Even then the path was not easy. Most of the debate centered on whether, in the new situation of freedom to worship that the Bill of Rights had created, the state through taxes should support all the churches or none. A host of influential people, led by Patrick Henry, were for the former, and in 1783-84 pressed for the adoption of a general assessment for the support of religion.[31] This seemed to have logic back of it, for the Bill of Rights had been pushed through by the growing power of the dissenting groups, and surely now they could expect to receive the state patronage that had hitherto gone to the Anglican Church alone. But Madison saw the danger and the unsound reasoning back of this proposal, and exposed it in a masterly paper, "Memorial and Remonstrance Against Religious Assessments."[32] Largely through the influence of this statement the plan for such an assessment was finally defeated by the Virginia legislature in 1785.

This left only the position that no church should be supported. Some years earlier Jefferson had written a document that incorporated this point of view, and now the Assembly passed it in 1785, and as the Statute of Religious Freedom it became a law in January, 1786.[33] This bill, together with a few subsequent actions to clean up some odds and ends of the old order, effectively disestablished the Church of England in Virginia.[34] Jefferson knew the profound significance of what had been done, for his authorship of the statute was, as his self-written epitaph at Monticello shows, one of the three accomplishments of which he was most proud, the other two being the authorship of the Declaration of Independence and the founding of the University of Virginia.[35] Taken together, the Bill of Rights and the Statute of Religious Freedom represent Virginia's monumental contribution to the cause of religious liberty in America.

The Federal Achievement

Once again the result in Virginia served as a precedent for the Federal Government when the Constitution was drafted in 1787. But whereas the Virginia achievement had been positive and direct, the work of the Constitutional Convention was negative and indirect. The majority of the delegates were accustomed to some form of state-church organic relationship in their home states, and yet it was palpably impossible for them to agree on some one establishment for the new Union. Congregational? Episcopal? Presbyterian? It could not be one of them, or any other.

Moreover, the writing of constitutions that had been undertaken in most states in the preceding ten years had usually included efforts at eliminating various degrees of organic connection, as well as making provisions, noted in Chapter II, for freedom to worship.[36] Since disestablishment was proceeding in many of the states, the task could safely be left alone; and where disestablishment was not proceeding it had to be left alone. Though there seems to have been much discussion of the matter, these points of view prevailed. Thus the prohibition of religious tests for Federal offices was the only notice the Constitution took of the question.[37] But the implication of this brief mention was clear: if religious tests were not to be allowed, then the Federal Government could no more set up a state church than it could prescribe or delimit individual worship.[38]

When the Constitution was taken to the various state ratifying conventions it soon became evident that the folks back home felt that the document did not go far enough, that a mere inference to be drawn from its one mention of religion was not sufficient. They felt they could trust themselves to do the right thing about both individual and institutional religion, but they could not trust their neighbors. Lest a combination of their neighbors in the new Federal Government foist on them principles or practices they abhorred, they clamored for a Federal Bill of Rights.[39]

Thus this was one of the first tasks facing Congress when it assembled in 1789. The question of wording came to be paramount, and Madison once again was in the thick of the fight. This time, however, he did not get all that he wanted, for he preferred a statement that would have provided for full religious liberty within all the states, as well as in the Federal Government.[40] The resulting clause in the First Amendment was a compromise between those who, like Madison, wanted a more comprehensive coverage, and those others who felt that no statement at all was needed, since the Federal Government did not possess any except specifically defined powers.[41] "Congress shall make no law respecting an establishment of religion," either to set one up or tear one down—this was Congress' disposition of the thorny phraseological problem, as ratified by the several states.[42]

Thus by negation Congress followed the Virginia lead, and in the process left the question to the states for final solution. These constitutional provisions, it is obvious, went only so far as to prevent the Federal Government from enacting legislation in a field that was reserved for the states themselves. Each state was free to maintain a religious establishment if it so desired, and several states did so in at least some form, notably Connecticut until 1818 and Massachusetts until 1833.[43] The struggles for disestablishment in those two old strongholds of Puritan theocracy were particularly bitter, but the moral influence of the rest of the country finally made itself felt. The present interpretation of the Fourteenth Amendment would suggest that the right of the states in this regard has now disappeared, for the courts are prepared to interpret the prohibition on the Federal Government as resting on the states as well.[44]

The Meaning of the Achievement

We must understand carefully what the development signified. The result in Virginia and later in other states and the Federal Government amounted to the establishment of the equality of all religious sects before the law. It meant that henceforth state and church would be mutually free of organic connection with each other. It was in Virginia that this development was first called "separation." Thus it is important to recognize that however the phrase has been misused in succeeding years, historically "separation" was synonymous with disestablishment, with equal legal status for all religious groups, and with full religious liberty.[45] The state was no longer to have any vested interests in the church nor the church in the state; each was to be organically independent of the other.

Yet the state did not thereby become opposed to the church; such a thing was unthinkable for America, for too often the leaders in one area were also the leaders in the other. Roger Williams, Samuel Davies, John Witherspoon, Isaac Backus, John Carroll, John Leland—all were churchmen who knew what they wanted in the political field, and all made great contributions to the new church-state relationship.[46] They would not have countenanced the creation of an unfriendly attitude between the two entities. Nor was such a creation in the minds of any of the great laymen of the movement, with the possible exception of Thomas Paine. The household names —Franklin, Washington, Patrick Henry, Jefferson, Madison— and the lesser known but influential figures, George Mason, Samuel Livermore, Charles Pinckney, and others, were operating on the basis of what they took to be good for the church as well as for the state.[47] Organic disconnection may sometimes be the work of a state hostile to religion, as it was later in France,[48] but in America it was brought about by both working together, often in opposition to elements within each.

On this point of responsibility the role of Jefferson and his deist leanings have occasionally been overemphasized. Exception can be taken to the nature of his influence on two counts. First of all, he was not as determinative for the actual occurrence as is supposed. Though he was the author of the Statute for Religious Freedom, he could not get it passed. He wrote it in 1777, but it was not passed until 1785, when, with Jefferson out of the country, the members of the dissenting denominations rallied to the leadership of Madison, a man of much more positive Christian faith.[49] Second, Jefferson's opposition to religion has been exaggerated. He intensely disliked sectarianism, and he believed deeply in the disestablishment that was brought about in Virginia and in the ensuing development in the Federal Government. But together with this his writings also show that his religious convictions, though often unorthodox, were profound and consciously motivating in his acts of statesmanship.[50]

Mention of Jefferson calls to mind the work of others only nominally attached to some church or not attached at all; Benjamin Franklin belongs in this group. That these people were numerous in late colonial times is well known, and that in the main they supported the various steps toward political freedom is widely attested. To give credit where it is due we must list the influence of the essentially unchurched as one more among the host of factors that combined to bring about disestablishment.[51] Yet their effectiveness was necessarily limited, as far as religious freedom was specifically concerned, because their attitude toward the church was suspect. Jefferson, Franklin, and others of their ilk helped to do the job, but the job was not accomplished by them.

Let it be stated categorically: we should never have had organic disconnection between church and state in this country if the nonconformist churches themselves had not wanted it, and struggled to bring it about, and if the leaders of the movement had not been able successfully to make the argument that the result would prove beneficial to the churches. That it has so proved is almost universally attested.[52] And this came to be recognized even by many opponents of the plan before they died. A good case in point is the churchman Lyman Beecher, who felt that the election day in Connecticut in 1818 that doomed the establishment was "as dark a day as ever I saw," but who by 1824 had changed his mind, for it proved to have been "the best thing that ever happened to the State of Connecticut."[53]

But if organic disconnection were not hostile, then some sort of association, though not organic, remained. Even as there were in colonial days degrees of connection, so in the post-Revolutionary days and on down to the present there have been degrees of disconnection. That is to say, though the position that the state may favor no church is fully and clearly established, there remain differences in both opinion and practice as to the extent to which the state may recognize organized religion as a whole. This is the battleground on which the struggle for religious liberty is now being fought in this country. The clamor of public discussion is loud and bitter, and the field is strewn with the forms of those felled by their own misunderstanding and partisanship. The whole conflict is so important for many issues of public concern in our day that we will devote special attention to it in later chapters.

Yet through all the din of present-day battle, one clear fact of the American practice emerges. Government, both state and Federal, has somehow managed the extremely difficult assignment of at one and the same time cutting organic ties and maintaining sympathetic associations with the churches. If the relationship in this country can correctly be described in one regard as the independence of church and state, there is another intangible sense in which it is also the interdependence of the two.

Postponing the difficulties that are involved, the attacks and the defenses, let us note simply the factual record, the variety of ways in which this relationship is manifest. The list is imposing: laws and law court decisions, such as already referred to in the preceding chapter, which recognize the claims of religious conscience; religious tests for jurors; tests of belief for witnesses and for officeholders; marriage laws; the use of prayer on official governmental occasions; Thanksgiving proclamations; Christmas and Easter observances; the study of the Bible and religion in tax-supported educational institutions; the use of "Year of our Lord" in official documents and of "In God We Trust" on stamps and coins; the presence of religious terminology in various constitutions; inaugural and other oaths; the presence of chaplains in governmental service; the exemption of church property from taxation; the provision of textbooks and bus rides for parochial school children; the subsidies to church-sponsored hospitals; the wording of the National Anthem and the Pledge of Allegiance; the social security benefits for church employees; and on and on and on.[54]

Some of these practices represent the willingness of government to give aid to religion, while others suggest the willingness to receive aid from religion. But whatever the nature of the contact, the recognition of religion involved is not, or is not presumed to be, a support of sectarianism. That is, we Americans are hereby not reneging on the organic disconnection of the state with one favored church that our forefathers achieved. Rather, we are serving notice in such actions —both in those that have been practiced uninterruptedly since the adoption of the Constitution and in those that have been begun in more recent times—that organic disconnection with one or another church did not mean the severance of all forms of relationship with institutional religion as a whole. I for one am not disposed to defend all the practices listed above. It may be, as certain writers say, that some of these are unwise ways for the government to give evidence of its impartial friendliness to religion.[55] But the contention is made that, wise or unwise, good or bad, these and other arrangements indicate that the government is not disabled from showing its support of nonsectarian religion.

And all this has been called "separation of church and state"! "Mutual independence" would be truer to history and present practice. But I am aware that my earlier plea to renounce "separation" will go unheeded. A better course, perhaps, is taken by Anson Phelps Stokes in the distinction he sets up between "unsympathetic or antagonistic separation" and "benevolent separation."[56] The latter, of course, is the term he applies to America, a situation in which "there is mutual understanding and sympathetic co-operation"[57] between the organically independent entities of state and church. We are stuck with the phrase. Then let us at least realize what it means, and to that end "benevolent separation" may help. It means something very close to what is increasingly seen as the Christian desire: the equality of all religious sects before the law, the absence of any hint of an establishment, and the practice of giving aid to, and receiving the ministrations of, nonsectarian religion.

CHAPTER V

The Misunderstanding
of Religious Freedom

The Role of the Protestants

THE three major aspects of religious freedom have come to be present in American life. We possess in remarkable degree the freedom to worship God as we see fit, the recognition by law of the supremacy of conscience, and both the independence and the interdependence of church and state. But things aren't as pretty as they seem. The trouble is that we don't know we've got them, we don't know the value of them, and we don't know what to do with them.

Perhaps the root of the difficulty is that we may not altogether believe in them. There is some historical ground for thinking this is so. Here we must be careful to give credit where credit is due, and to evaluate justly the contribution of various groups to the development of both the practice and the theory of freedom.

In some Catholic circles it has recently become fashionable to point out that Catholics played a major role in the struggle for religious liberty in America.[1] Now one has no disposition to underestimate Cecil Calvert's partly successful plan for toleration in the seventeenth century, or John Carroll's work toward adjusting the ideas of Catholics to the new concepts of freedom in the eighteenth century. Archbishop Carroll, as the first Roman prelate in the states, supported American independence and gave his sanction to the guarantees of religious liberty that the new nation provided; but Stokes concludes his appreciation of Carroll's work by the recognition that "there is no evidence that he personally took any large part in bringing about these guarantees."[2]

Even less influential, if at all, were the ideas of two European Jesuits, Francisco Suarez and Roberto Bellarmine. For a time some Catholic apologists were inclined to make out that Jefferson, for one, had got many of his notions about religious freedom from these Catholic sources,[3] but in recent years even the Catholics have joined in the explosion of what has been called "the Bellarmine myth."[4] The development in America was not brought about by the Catholics.

A much more plausible theory is that the accomplishment was the result of the wave of free thought stirring in secular circles in the seventeenth and eighteenth centuries.[5] Here is where John Locke again enters our picture. It is generally recognized that Jefferson, Madison, and other Revolutionary leaders got much of their political philosophy from Locke and other lovers of liberty who preceded and followed him. We must weigh carefully the effect of this attribution. First of all, we need to recognize two ways in which the position is sound. It goes without saying that Jefferson and particularly Madison were influential in large degree for the American creation. Further, by virtue of their having been influenced by the deists, freethinkers, and secular political philosophers generally, they possessed a profound belief in what they were doing as the soundest theory to follow as well as the best practical measure.[6]

Yet when those two facts are recognized, other factors suggest that the hypothesis can be carried too far. Some of the factors have been noted in other connections: that John Locke was not a secularist in the sense of opponent, nor even in the sense of neutralist, as far as religion was concerned; and that the role Jefferson played in the practical struggle has sometimes been exaggerated.[7]

Other realizations are important: John Locke and most of his train of followers did not carry the implications of his position as far as his American disciples found it necessary and wise to do. Basing his thought on that of Richard Hooker and John Milton, Locke, like them, went only so far as to counsel freedom of worship and its attendant civil liberties—not to press for organic disconnection between church and state.[8] Moreover, the contact of late eighteenth century European thinkers with the Americans worked more often in the opposite direction than has commonly been supposed. French thinkers were influenced by American thought and development; and the American Revolution, both in fact and in theory, be it remembered, antedated the French Revolution.[9]

This is to say that the religious liberty of America was an indigenous development, touched but not directed by European forces of theory and practice. Jefferson, Madison, and others, including Tom Paine, drank deep of the well of liberal sentiment abroad, but they were themselves creative thinkers, and based their concepts on the current domestic scene as much as or more than on the philosophies of foreigners.[10] Moreover, they did not do the job alone, and in the doing of it they did not oppose religious ideas. The conclusion is that secularism and deism, like Catholicism, was not responsible for the religious freedom of the new America.

Then what was responsible? Protestantism. To make it even more precise, Dissent. To be sure, many who were devoted to the established churches joined heartily in the fight for freedom. This was true to some extent in New England, and to a very large extent in Virginia.[11] In fact, the laity of the Virginia Anglican Church, some quite loyal, some only nominally related, furnished a disproportionate number of the leaders of the fight. Leadership came also from the unchurched population, as we have noted earlier. But the leaders had to have a following, and the overwhelming mass of those who joined the cause were dissenters—Baptists and Presbyterians; Episcopalians and Congregationalists living outside the bounds of their church-state colonies; Dutch Reformed, Lutherans, Quakers, Mennonites, and members of other small sects; and those converts of Whitefield and the Great Awakening who became Methodists.[12] Of this group the Presbyterians and Baptists led all the rest, both numerically and in their fervor of devotion.

This is particularly noticeable in the crucial conflict in Virginia.[13] Both the Bill of Rights and the Statute of Religious Freedom were enacted through the generalship of Madison and his helpers, with Jefferson playing the strategist's role; but the privates in the ranks were the dissenters. And if there had been no large and determined army there would have been no fight. The victory for religious liberty was a compound of many forces, the work of many diverse people, the outgrowth of many varied movements. But that one element that could not possibly have been spared, that one factor more effective than any of the rest, was the participation of the dissenting Protestants.

Yet there is shame as well as glory in this realization. If it was Protestantism that was most instrumental in the development it was also Protestantism that was in greatest opposition.[14] Moreover, the opponents came not alone from the supporters of existing state churches; others as well looked askance on ideas of freedom, others who, though they did not then possess what they took to be the blessings of an establishment, were loath to give up the hope of a state-church connection that their European heritage had led them to think was sound. But they were caught by the necessities of the situation in which they found themselves at the time of the formation of the Republic.[15]

In fact, both sides were caught. And the dilemma was as if they were saying to themselves, "How can we have what we want, and yet be assured that others won't thereby be able to force us to have what we don't want?" The real obstacle was the number and diversity of the sects. In this situation freedom proved to be less fearsome than establishment, or than its liberal half-brother, toleration. But it was a matter of degree, and there were many who were afraid of freedom.

The result, then, was not a clean-cut victory in a fight in which the issues were clear; rather, it was a compromise in a struggle in which the issues were confused. Strangely, the obstacle proved to be the key to the successful outcome: diversity compelled concessions. Religious freedom was secured primarily by the nonconformist Protestants; but, humbling admission that it is, it was gained not so much by intention and conviction as by accident and compromise.[16]

The Legacy of Misunderstanding

The inevitable accompaniment of such a settlement was that the Protestants did not completely understand what they had gained. For many, the result seemed to lie in the practical realm of manners rather than the theoretical realm of morals. Though it was not true for many of the leaders, yet for the mass on whose support the success of the venture depended, practice had outrun theory. Deists, freethinkers, and other secularists had undergirded their program with a philosophy of the natural rights of man. The many loyal churchmen among the leaders had rooted their conception of such rights in their faith in God. Thus the leaders, whether secular or religious in their motivations, were conscious of possessing a political philosophy that called for the new regime. But it is to be questioned that this philosophizing seeped down very far; for most of those who were instrumental in bringing in the new day, theory had to catch up with practice.

The people, if not their leaders, had fought not so much *for* something as against something else; they had struggled against the constraints of the colonial society. Thus they were prepared to understand something of the rights that had been gained through the victory, but not the responsibilities. They fought for their own rights in the colonies to which they were attached, but there was nowhere near as much interest in the rights of others far distant, or of a different turn of mind. Few of them seemed to be able to attain the breadth of vision of a Jefferson or a Franklin. And thus the people interpreted the new order almost altogether in terms of what it meant to them—the elimination of their own disabilities—and to their churches—the disestablishment, or relinquishment of the favored role, of the state-supported church.[17]

Many of them had neither the knowledge nor the inclination to look at the other side of the picture—that this was a great enabling, as well as a disabling step, for all individual worshippers and all groups. They noted the tangible ties that were cut, but not the intangible ties that remained. How easy it was, then, for them to speak of the development as "the separation of church and state," forgetting that that was only one aspect of religious freedom, and a partial rendering of that one. Rights but not responsbilities, independence but not interdependence—this was the heart of the misunderstanding.

And this was tragic, for it meant that religious liberty came to be conceived simply as a glorious expediency. Glorious it was; for the oppressive past, stretching back through the centuries, had been overthrown. But expediency it also was; for the full catalogue of principles that were involved were diluted and turned to the protection of personal advantages. Misunderstanding bred expediency, and expediency in turn bred further misunderstanding.

The confusion is still with us. We still do not know what our religious freedom really means. To be sure, the historical development is sufficiently clear to enable us to draw such general conclusions as were suggested in the three preceding chapters. Moreover, present-day construction through custom and juridical decision shows our almost full acceptance of the heritage in its first aspect, that of freedom to worship, and of our growing appreciation of its second, that of the recognition of the supremacy of conscience. Most of the confusion, therefore, centers on the third aspect, the relationship of church and state.

That this is so is not to be marvelled at. As human beings, we are more easily self-centered than selfless; we would rather deal with blacks and whites than grays; we trust ourselves sooner than we trust others or than others trust us; and we are quicker to negate than to affirm. All these human traits combine to make us more susceptible to partial understandings of religious freedom in general and the relationship of church and state in particular, and to make us less willing to undergo the careful balancing of the component parts of those developments through which alone a complete understanding can be gained. But marvel or no, our imperfect understanding is deplorable, for it means that we are thereby setting up unnecessary impediments to America's entering into its full heritage.

Everson and McCollum

This confusion is well illustrated by a series of recent court decisions having to do with public education in various aspects —the area in which the problem comes to sharpest focus today. The two most widely discussed are the Everson and McCollum cases. In the Everson case the point at immediate issue was as to whether New Jersey could pay bus fares for parochial school children, as a state statute of 1941 provided. The payment was challenged on the grounds that it threatened religious freedom and "the separation of church and state." Winding its way through the courts, it was decided by the Supreme Court in 1947, which supported the New Jersey law by a vote of five to four.[18] But the closeness of the vote is only a minor part of the evidence of confused thinking, both in the Court and in the public at large.

There were three opinions, one for the majority, written by

Justice Black, and two dissenting. Justice Jackson was the author of one dissent, concurred in by Justice Frankfurter, and Justice Rutledge wrote the other, concurred in by Justices Jackson, Frankfurter, and Burton. Jackson confined his attention almost wholly to the issue at hand, but based his dissent on matters of church-state relations. Rutledge produced a long and remarkable document on the history and interpretation of Constitutional provisions for church-state separation. Using Jefferson's famous word about the "wall," and various statements of Madison, he took a rigid and extreme position, attempting to show that

We have staked the very existence of our country on the faith that complete separation between the State and religion is best for the State and best for religion.[19]

But the majority opinion went him one better. Lest any should think that he was not prepared to defend "separation," Justice Black also quoted Jefferson and cited Madison, and added the now-famous statement,

Neither a state nor the Federal Government can set up a church. Neither can pass laws which aid one religion, aid all religions, or prefer one religion over another.[20]

Applying this declaration to the problem at hand, and finding a partial precedent in the Louisiana textbook case of 1930,[21] the majority approved free bus rides for parochial school children!

Then the flood of confusion in the public mind burst on the Court. Those who approved the decision, mostly Catholics, deplored the reasoning that led to it. Those who approved the reasoning deplored the decision. Everybody got into the act, and either reasoning or decision was stoutly defended or, more often, roundly castigated, by lawyers, by churchmen, and by the general public.[22] That the reader may know where I stand, I deplore both reasoning and decision—as was noted above, negation comes easier than affirmation!

But one is more important than the other. The decision was on a specific point of the application of the principle, and is admittedly a difficult and debatable matter. I personally cannot see how the reasoning of the Court that the Constitution prevents giving aid to one religion can then be made to justify a program that does substantially that. The same problem arises in connection with allowing free textbooks to Catholic children in Louisiana. But I for one am willing to admit the difficulty of the immediate application, and thus am willing to grant the possibility that in the eyes of others the decision may seem sound.

The reasoning back of it, however, is a much more significant item. Note Rutledge's use of the term, "complete separation," and Black's insertion of the phrase, "aid all religions," between the other two acts the Government may not perform, "aid one religion," and "prefer one religion over another." The completeness of the "wall," and the prohibition against aiding all religions as well as just one, are conclusions drawn from a partial reading of history and practice, including the intention of the founding fathers. This is emphasizing only one aspect of the American pattern of relationship between church and state, the disabling side.

But my calling attention to the matter is not so much for the purpose of re-arguing the issues pro and con—for that was attempted briefly in preceding chapters—but to point out the misunderstanding that the Everson case brought forth. Disabling reasoning led to an enabling decision; and people were inevitably mixed up. If the decision was wrong, then how easy it was to conclude that the reasoning had not been disabling enough, that it ought to be even more restrictive. So ran the thinking of nearly all commentators except the Catholics.[23]

And then came the McCollum case. Since 1940 the public schools of Champaign, Illinois, had sanctioned a "released-time" program of religious education in the school buildings, with children attending classes taught by their respective religious guides, Protestants, Catholics, and a Jew. Though the instruction was voluntary, a Mrs. Vashti McCollum objected, in 1945, that hardship was being imposed on her little son Terry. His not attending any class—for Mrs. McCollum was an atheist—left him open to the ridicule of his fellows. The nub of the matter—so the contention ran—was that the social pressure in support of the religious instruction was so strong that a *de facto* if not *de jure* "establishment of religion" had been created. Thus the First Amendment as extended to the states by the Fourteenth, came into the picture; and by the time the Supreme Court heard the case, the question of the hardship on Terry had been lost in the shuffle of debate on the larger Constitutional issue. By a vote of eight to one the Supreme Court decided in 1948 that the Champaign plan was unconstitutional.[24]

It had been freely predicted that this would be the decision, for both the reasoning of the justices in the Everson case and the direction of most of the public clamor about that judgment, including the legal reviews of it, pointed to such an outcome.[25] But the justices still had a difficult time. There were three statements on the side of the majority; the Court opinion was written by Justice Black, and concurring opinions were written by Justices Frankfurter and Jackson. Justices Rutledge and Burton concurred in Black's opinion, and Justices Jackson, Rutledge and Burton joined in Justice Frankfurter's opinion. Justice Reed, who wrote the dissenting opinion, was the only one who escaped the entanglement. Almost everything got in the picture; if not the proverbial kitchen sink, at least Robert Frost, for Frankfurter concluded by misunderstanding Frost's meaning in his phrase, "Good fences make good neighbors"![26]

Justice Reed buttressed his dissent by reference to both history and custom. He wrote:

The prohibition of enactments respecting the establishment of religion do not bar every friendly gesture between church and state. It is not an absolute prohibition. . . . Devotion to the great principle of religious liberty should not lead us into a rigid interpretation of the constitutional guarantee that conflicts with accepted habits of our people.[27]

But his was a mild argument. Reviewing the Virginia and Federal struggles he concluded,

The phrase "an establishment of religion" may have been intended by Congress to be aimed only at a state church.[28]

Supporters of Reed's position have pointed out the weakening effect of his phrase, "may have been."[29]

Yet for Reed to have gone so far is remarkable in the light of the overwhelming pressure of his colleagues. For all their differences of emphasis among each other, they combined in reiterating the declarations in the Everson case; and now, ready to apply that reasoning, plumped powerfully for keeping Jefferson's "wall," as Black said, "high and impregnable."[30] Frankfurter wrote,

Separation means separation, not something less. Jefferson's metaphor in describing the relation between Church and State speaks . . . not of a fine line easily overstepped. . . . It is the Court's duty to enforce this principle in its full integrity.[31]

But strangely, no sweeping conclusion was drawn from such sweeping argument; on the contrary, judgment as distinct from the reasoning back of it, was expressed only on the particular situation in Champaign;

others may be found unexceptionable. We do not now attempt to weigh in the Constitutional scale every separate detail or various combination of factors which may establish a valid "released time" program.[32]

Once again the Court had labored like a mountain. This time, at least they had had no abortion; they brought forth a mouse.

And a very puzzling mouse it was. Seldom had such an unbending decision been so flexible. As if the bewilderment about the Everson case had not been enough, the Court's new stand effectively scattered the elements that had made up the majority reaction to that former judgment. The variety of opinions turned on the following questions: If the Champaign plan is unconstitutional, what about other "released-time" programs that differ in details? (This of course provoked the side issue, What good are they, anyway?) What changes must be made in existing programs, in order to have them conform to the Court's judgment?[33] Must the Court pass on each type? If the Court does "not now attempt to weigh . . . every separate detail," does that mean that the Court feels that it is its duty to do so eventually? Is the Court either empowered or fit to act as a national Board of Education?[34]

More general questions arose: Since the Court in its opinions expressly took both the Everson and the McCollum cases out of the area of public education alone, and into the area of church-state relations in general, can government ever have anything to do with religion? How can it fail to? What did Jefferson and Madison really intend? Whatever their intentions, what did the Constitution actually establish? What is the principle, and what is "its full integrity," that the Court is in duty bound to enforce?[35]

The Zorach Case

Such questions produced scurrying hither and yon; in action as well as comment confusion was prevalent. Various states took various courses with respect to their released-time programs, and some states did nothing, waiting for further clarification.[36]

Such clarification was supposedly offered in *Zorach v. Clauson*, a 1952 decision of the Supreme Court that ruled on the legality of New York's "released-time" plan.[37] By a vote of six to three the Court found enough difference between the New York and Illinois practices to warrant approval in this case, though rejection in the other. The major difference was that the New York program was not conducted within public school buildings, though on school time. Justice Douglas wrote the majority opinion, and Justices Black, Frankfurter, and Jackson each wrote dissents. The puzzlement of the populace before the verdict is well shown by the astonishing assortment of individuals and groups that presented briefs on one side or the other. These included arguments by the attorney generals of no fewer than eight states.[38]

After the verdict the perplexity remains. To be sure some matters were cleared up, perhaps two quite important ones, as we shall note in the next chapter. But once again the Court had given the impression, on the one hand of stating an august principle in rigid form, and on the other of quibbling over the implications. If the principle were as plain as the McCollum case suggested, why was the McCollum case not more decisive? Why could it not cover the Zorach case as well? Justice Jackson's dissent posed the problem querulously:

The distinction attempted between that case and this is trivial, almost to the point of cynicism, magnifying its nonessential details. . . . The wall which the Court was professing to erect between Church and State has become even more warped and twisted than I expected. Today's judgment will be more interesting to students of psychology and of the judicial processes than to students of constitutional law.[39]

—A comment which could apply to his own as well as to the contrary point of view!

This is almost exactly the point we are trying to make. For the purpose of this discussion is to show not so much that one or another decision was sound or unsound, but that the ways of arguing all these cases were confused, and in turn spread confusion. As to my own opinion, simply that of a layman rather than of a lawyer, I think the verdicts in both the McCollum and the Zorach cases are sound, but that the reasoning back of them, including dissenting as well as majority opinions, is garbled.

But I am ready to give ground in my reaction to the verdicts, for admittedly they are debatable matters; it is the declarations, as exposing the philosophy underlying the verdicts, that are significant for any long-term solution to the problem. Everson, McCollum, and Zorach posed two kinds of difficulty, one having to do with the understanding of the principle and the other with the application of the principle to the perplexing issue at hand.

The second kind of difficulty will always be present; and for that reason I for one am prepared to admit that the particular verdict in each case might have been different, and at least in the Everson case ought to have been different.

But the danger is in the manifest presence of the first difficulty in the minds of the justices of the Court and of the people of the land. In all three cases the Court opinions did not grapple solely with the awkward problem of application; they got worse bogged down in the principle itself. They saw the principle only in its negative or restrictive aspect, and this made their problem of application even more troublesome. If their verdict was to be permissive, as it was in the Everson and Zorach cases, then they were called to perform handsprings of adjustment from a negative principle to an affirmative decision. If their verdict was to be prohibitive in one specific situation, as it was in the McCollum case, then they experienced discomfiture in showing how a conclusive principle could produce a generally inconclusive verdict.

The root of the difficulty is in their not understanding that the principle has an enabling as well as a disabling aspect. By omitting the enabling side they have misread both American history and American practice; consequently they have no justification in their own faulty premises for such permissive action as—in spite of that—they then proceed to consider. One is grateful that the Court will at least consider permissive action in this storm-tossed area of church-state relations; one is deeply disturbed that the Court does not base such consideration on the available and valid foundation, the American principle of the relationship of church and state that stresses both organic disconnection and sympathetic association between the two.

CHAPTER VI

The Price
of Misunderstanding

The Catholic Attack

THE most dangerous thing about this misunderstanding is that various extremists seek to take advantage of the resulting confusion in order to press some particular interpretation or desire of their own.

In one direction are the Catholics, joined on occasion by a few others who are still wedded to some theory of establishment. Their brand of extremism is to the effect that, since ideally church and state should be one, or that each should be an organic arm of support for the other in its own sphere, then though the ideal cannot be reached in present-day America we should approach it as closely as we can. That is, in terms of specific programs, we should make tax money available to the parochial schools and colleges, we should finance various kinds of so-called auxiliary services for Catholic school children, we should establish a regular ambassadorship at the Vatican, and in every other possible way we should use the power of the state for the benefit of the church.[1]

Yet the Catholic position is not easy to summarize, for they follow a devious line. On occasion they fight as hard as the atheists for the complete elimination of all mention of religion in the public schools;[2] and then they follow up with the self-righteous charge, "Look how godless our public schools are!"[3] When it seems to their advantage they can take constructive part in some nonsectarian program;[4] and then on other occasion they can point out that nonsectarian means inescapably anti-Catholic, and thus they can have nothing to do with it.[5] They can ask for concessions, leaving the implication that such support is all they want;[6] and then if the concessions are given, they can point out that their own theory of church-state relations requires them to have control as well as support.[7]

The trouble is not so much that they find it impossible to be loyal both to America and to Rome as they understand the demands of each in respect to religious freedom. It *is* possible in their minds, as their record in military, political, and other forms of public life amply attests. The trouble is, rather, that they find it difficult to conceive of a conflict of loyalty between the two; and further, that when such tensions arise, as they inevitably do, they seek to bend the position of one to fit the formula of the other, rather than to admit the conflict.[8] Thus Rome often gives way to America—but that danger is not part of our worry here. The opposite danger does concern us all; they would sometimes have America give way to Rome.

The operation of this policy is usually evident in local situations—taking over a public school board, allowing nuns to teach in a public school, and various other limited but clear infractions of the principle of impartiality.[9] Sometimes the Catholic aims are given forthright expression, as in Father Ryan's books on political science,[10] or Cardinal Spellman's squabble with Mrs. Roosevelt.[11] Increasingly the Catholic lobby has pressed for or defended legislative or executive action in Washington and other governmental centers that would be advantageous to Catholics alone,[12] and if objection is raised the Catholic press has been quick to cry, "Prejudice!"[13]

But these procedures sooner or later get recognized for what they are, namely, the effort on the part of Catholic leaders to secure special benefits from the hands of the state. More dangerous is the more moderate approach reflected in recent writings of such Catholic authors as Wilfred Parsons[14] and James M. O'Neill,[15] though often O'Neill's language, as distinct from his thesis, is far from moderate.

The argument and strategy of Parsons' volume, *The First Freedom*, and O'Neill's two books, *Religion and Education under the Constitution*, and *Catholicism and American Freedom*, are essentially the same. By picking and choosing among the relevant historical references they construct a hypothesis of religious freedom that stresses the permissive aspect of the relationship of church and state and de-emphasizes the restrictive aspect. Arguing with justice that "there is no such great American principle" as "complete separation of Church and State,"[16] they make this realization serve their own ends of justifying programs that imply that there is no separation of any kind. The unwary can be caught in their argument, for they use it to warrant such time-honored customs as prayer before legislative bodies and the presence of chaplains in the armed forces.[17] But they do not stop there, or even with those matters of borderline decision such as were raised in the Everson, McCollum, and Zorach cases. To follow their full thesis would require the state eventually to aid one religion at the expense of others, and whatever else the American principle means it has clearly set its face against any such system.

A brief elaboration may be useful. Parsons is disturbed at the

McCollum decision, for he sees it as seeking to establish some
new American principle of church-state relationships rather
than merely enunciating an old one. This new principle is "'the
shibboleth of separation of church and state."[18] Tracing the
American development from the framing of the Constitution
down to the present, he argues not alone that separation "does
not mean what it says," but also that it "does not mean anything at all."[19] The two key words to a correct understanding
are "distinction and co-operation"; and he seeks to show that the
kind of "distinction" between church and state that we have in
America is exactly the sort that Catholics have always upheld.[20]

Up to this point there is much in Parson's argument with
which the present writer is in agreement—though much else, I
believe, in which the emphasis or interpretation should be different. But it is from this point on, as Parsons explores the meaning of his second term, "co-operation," that the crucial differences between us become clear. Parsons would have "co-operation" justify various kinds of special help to parochial schools.[21]
But when he maintains that "the Catholic parochial school is a
true public school,"[22] he is simply ignoring one of the essential
meanings attached to the term "public school" in this country,
namely, that it is under public control. He says: "When the
state grants support to a Catholic school in some way it is not
because it is Catholic; it is because the students are members
of our society."[23] If his were truly a selfless concern for students
of all religious faiths and of none, then something might be said
for it; but even in that event the state would have to wink at the
fact that help would be given to one or another denomination—
to any that chose to establish a system of parochial schools.
This is to require the state to be forgetful of Madison's "Remon-

strance" against Patrick Henry's proposal to subsidize various denominations; and by that measure it would depart from American policy and practice.

O'Neill's Bias

O'Neill's is a more detailed argument, which he buttresses with much historical material and various useful appendices consisting of the reprinting of relevant documents. He too takes his cue from the majority opinions in the McCollum case, which he labels "semantic and historical nonsense."[24] The fault of the Supreme Court justices in both the Everson and McCollum cases, he believes, is that they misunderstood the meaning of the phrase "an establishment of religion" in the First Amendment. In respect to the Everson opinions, both majority and minority, he says, "The Supreme Court's magnification of Jefferson's wall is fantastic. It has no relation to any reality of either law or fact."[25] McCollum is even worse, for that decision represents "an elaborate debauchery of the First Amendment."[26] All that the First Amendment meant to do, he says, was to prevent Congress from setting up "a formal, legal union of a single church or religion with government,"[27] and thus the way was left open for various types of association short of "formal, legal union." O'Neill supports this thesis by reference at length to Jefferson's and Madison's positions, and the history of Congressional action, the record of the Supreme Court up to the Everson case, and "the practices of the several states."[28]

Thus there is much in the bare bones of O'Neill's argument to educe our sympathy, but much else calls for rejection. Even when one is inclined to agree, the extravagance of his language raises suspicions that something more is involved than simply a disinterested endeavor to set the justices straight. The harsh words noted in the preceding paragraph are only a beginning: he actually suggests that the Supreme Court in the McCollum case has substituted "life under a dictatorship for democracy and constitutional government."[29] This is not a slip of the pen, for somehow the whole question is a matter of "civil liberties" and their retention; he writes, "Everyone will lose his freedom if he leaves the job of protecting it to congressmen and Supreme Court judges."[30]

Why? What is back of O'Neill's diatribe? Most of the time he limits his discussion rigidly to the task at hand, that of exposing the ignorance, or worse, of the Supreme Court.[31] But now and then the reader gets an inkling of his own desires, and of the way in which he would interpret the American relationship of church and state if he had the chance. For example, though he belabors the Court for its "false history and biography, garbled quotations, and fallacious reasoning" in the Everson case, he feels that the outcome "is the only possible decision which is consistent with the language and meaning of the First Amendment. . . ."[32] He approves, therefore, bus rides for Catholic school children at public expense; this is only one illustration of the "federal aid to parochial schools" that he favors.[33] Again, those who oppose United States representation at the Vatican are invoking a "spurious principle" or engaging in rank prejudice.[34] While holding such opinions he yet argues —undoubtedly with sincerity—that Catholics seek no special privileges.[35]

The resolution of this conflict lies in his belief "that the First Amendment had nothing whatever to do with any theory of public financing or the propriety or impropriety of using public funds for any purpose whatever."[36] "Nothing whatever . . . whatever"? But there could hardly be "establishment" without some measure of financial support; and when Congress is barred from setting up an establishment, it is barred from giving financial aid to any one denomination in preference to another. Though O'Neill rightly points out that the Federal Government can, and does, use "public funds in support of religion,"[37] he would like to pretend that the possibility of support for all religions, or for nonsectarian religion, means that the First Amendment implies no limitations at all in the use of public funds. This is where his Catholic bias shows through; and the fact that the reasoning of the justices at which he complains endangers not only legitimate associations of church and state but also questionable types of support that Catholics especially desire, may be the explanation for his intemperate language.

Since it happens that Catholics are usually the protagonists for the extreme permissive position, one who is himself not a Catholic must seek to make plain that his disagreement with their interpretation arises not because it is they who hold it but because of the position itself. O'Neill deplores what he takes to be "a widespread attempt to make this a Catholic vs. a Protestant fight,"[38] and I share his feeling. Yet, though personalities should not enter the picture, and religious wars should be a thing of the past, one of the inescapable facts is that Catholics want special concessions, and often get them; and as we have seen, seek to interpret the American policy in church-state relationships so as to justify them. It must be stated therefore, without malice, yet with all candor, that the Catholic desire to receive peculiar favors would be, if it were successful, a subversion of the American principle.

The Anti-Catholic Attack

The opposite extreme—antithetical not so much to the more plausible Parsons and O'Neill as to Catholic extravagance that seldom receives such respectable argumentation—is represented by the agonized outbursts of the agnostics and atheists. Two typical examples are the book by Frank Swancara, *Obstruction of Justice by Religion*,[39] and an article in the *Yale Law Journal* by B. H. Hartogensis, "Denial of Equal Rights to Religious Minorities and Non-Believers in the United States."[40] Swancara's subtitle reflects his position: "A Treatise on Religious Barbarities of the Common Law, and a Review of Judicial Oppressions of the Non-Religious in the United States." Such folks would throw out the baby of the intangible interest with the dirty bath-water of the tangible tie, contending that the baby was thoroughly dirty too. They maintain that separation should be not only "complete" in organic matters but require such a degree of neutrality as to make it in fact—though not by their admission—hostile to all religion.[41] That such a notion does not fit the facts of history or present practice goes without saying.

But their contention has this one useful result: it calls notice to the fact that in America, unlike some other countries in which disestablishment was undertaken in antagonism to the church, religious freedom is neither freedom from religion nor freedom for irreligion. To give complete freedom to the atheist is necessarily in some measure to proscribe the freedom of believers.[42] We cannot have it both ways; and America has chosen its pattern, to be both friendly and impartial to religion. Within this framework the atheist has as much liberty as can be made consistent with the freedom of the believer, but no more. This we need to recognize; and noting, need to be alert to grant the atheist all the liberty that is possible, including certainly the freedom not to worship, and to refuse only those attempts on his part to encroach on our own.[43]

The comparable position to that of Parsons and O'Neill is held by a widely assorted group of able men who have become disturbed at the Catholic attempt in polemic and practice to weaken the American principle. Alarmed at the increasing outspokenness of Catholic writers and the growing evidences of partisan activity, they have joined together to form such groups as "Protestants and Other Americans United for the Separation of Church and State," and "The Institute of Church and State," both founded in 1948 as a direct response to the Everson decision.[44] In recent years a spate of perturbed studies dealing with one or many aspects of the problem has come from authors as competent and diverse as the following: Paul Blanshard, R. Freeman Butts, Joseph Martin Dawson, Alvin W. Johnson, Conrad H. Moehlman, Leo Pfeffer, and V. T. Thayer.[45] Their degrees of distress are as varied as their causes for it and their expressions of it.

Yet certain clear arguments underlie the work of all the authors mentioned. First of all, they rightly accuse the Catholics of picking and choosing among the relevant historical references, and then they themselves choose and pick. Arguing with justice that " 'an establishment of religion' . . . is a threat to religious freedom and to the American tradition of democracy,"[46] they make this position cover what is called "multiple" as well as single establishment, and then interpret "multiple establishment" as being synonymous with and referring to nearly all forms of "co-operation."[47] The unwary can likewise be caught in this argument, for some of them will admit that the ban on co-operation should not extend so far as to prohibit such time-honored customs as prayer before legislative bodies and the presence of chaplains in the armed forces.[48] But they do not always draw the line there, and certainly they do not consider that matters raised in the Everson, McCollum, and Zorach cases should be borderline decisions. To follow their full thesis would require the state eventually to recognize no relation at all to organized religion; and whatever else the American principle means, it has clearly set its face against any such system.

But we must not content ourselves merely with recapturing the phraseology of our rebuttal to the Catholics.[49] For several reasons this is a more serious challenge than even the Catholic one. First, though both sides remind us of the story of the camel with his nose in the tent, the complete separationists represent a smaller nose and a smaller camel, and thus are harder to detect at work; but camel-like they can still overturn and occupy the tent. That is, they can stand against visible Catholic invasions of the American system in such fashion as invisibly to distort it, and thus eventually work its destruction. The Catholic invasion is the larger camel, but the "defense" against it may be more dangerous to the habitation.

Second, and to change the figure, though both are grinding special axes, the Catholic axe is sharper. This is to say that the Catholics clearly have something to gain from their argument, but the contrary position is seemingly more disinterested. In fact, it is undoubtedly more disinterested, for many in the group, particularly the Protestants, are simply basing their position on mistaken premises.

Third, the Catholic danger is not as large, because they need to inveigh less against present practice if not against theory. The pressure to oppose what the complete separationists feel is faulty practice may easily persuade them to adopt an even more rigorous theory.

All this leads to the final and most tragic reason: the "Protestants and Other Americans United . . ." in what they take to be a great crusade are allowing themselves to be outmaneuvered by the Catholics. Often it is the Catholics who call the tune, and the Protestants and others merely protest. Not all the protesting is directed at the Catholics themselves, and in general the amenities of social intercourse are preserved. Rather, complaint is often lodged against what they take to be apathy, that is, against the non-Catholic population who simply will not become alarmed at the supposedly imminent collapse of the American system. Thus the complete separationists often look on those of us who take a middle road, who hold in mind the enabling as well as disabling aspects of the church-state relationship, as their opponents. This is deplorable, for it indicates that they have worked themselves into a cul-de-sac of misunderstanding. Their response to the Catholics' departure on a twisting path is to march off, in the other direction, toward a dead end.

Let us look at a few examples. We will begin with Paul Blanshard, who has had the widest reading of any of the authors mentioned above, and whose books are most sharply aimed at the Catholics. But, though his concern is with the growth of Catholic power in nearly every area of life, the question of church-state relations is ever-present, and he is particularly conscious of the problem in the field of education. In fact, here is the nub of the matter: ". . . the outcome of the struggle between American democracy and the Catholic hierarchy depends upon the survival and expansion of the public school."[50]

Blanshard believes in "separation" and contends that, no matter what Catholics may say on occasion, they do not believe in it because they cannot.[51] In his chapters on "Education and the Catholic Mind" and "Public Schools and Public Money," he gives evidence of various ways in which Catholics have tried to weaken or destroy the pattern of "separation." Though he never discusses the meaning he gives the phrase, it becomes clear in his opposition to Catholic actions that he himself holds to a rigid interpretation. "Separation of church and state in educational matters" means not only that the public schools must be free from denominational control and sectarian activities, but that, further, they must be viewed "as secular institutions divorced from distinctively religious teaching."[52] What shall we do to stop the Catholics' "step-by-step gains"? We must construct "a wall of separation" and "make it real with no compromise."[53]

All our other authors in this category follow a similar line; in differing degrees, overtly or tacitly, they take the Catholics to task. In greater or lesser measure they see the peril to the public school. They vary in the extent to which they call history to their aid. But all stand together in their interpretation of the American principle of the relationship of church and state. The Federal achievement meant not just the equality of all religious sects before the law but "complete separation," "absolute separation," "rigid separation," "eternal separation" of church and state; as Johnson and Yost phrase it, "a complete emancipation of civil and religious agencies from each other."[54]

To "Protect" the Public School

Of all these writers Johnson has least to say concerning Catholics. That he is worried about them, however, is evident from his references to certain practices peculiarly characteristic of them that he says are "repugnant to the American people."[55] His major interest is with education; and both in his earlier volume, *Legal Status of Church-State Relationships in the United States,* and in its revision, *Separation of Church and State in the United States,* with Frank H. Yost as co-author, he gives valuable information concerning such perplexing educational practices as Bible reading, dismissed- and released-time programs of religious education, credit for religious instruction, the wearing of religious garb in public schools, and free textbooks and transportation for parochial school pupils. He looks askance on all these activities, not merely on those which aid simply one denomination; and his grounds for doing so rest in his understanding of the meaning of "separation." His brief excursion in history discloses only the disabling aspect of the American principle. Thus his wish is father to the thought when he says, without any qualification, "The teaching of religion in the public schools is now unconstitutional."[56] Notice the restrictive wording in the following sweeping conclusions:

Any alliance or bond joining the church and the state in their separate functions, in their separate and distinct spheres of operation, is not only injurious to both but forebodes evil to all concerned.[57]

The state, that is, the people acting in their organic capacity through the machinery of law, says to all religious sects, to all antireligionists, and to all classes of citizens that its position with respect to the public schools is one of absolute and impartial "neu-

trality" toward all religious doctrines, whether they be drawn from
the Bible or another source. . . . In short, its purpose is secular education with no meddling in the province of the church. . . . It is
only as such a position is taken that the principles and ideals upon
which our government is founded, namely, the complete separation
of church and state, may be maintained.[58]

V. T. Thayer, too, is concerned with public education. In
his latest book he is disturbed about what he calls *The Attack
upon the American Secular School*. Catholics are involved in
this attack, for they are both opposed to the secular idea and
desirous of securing special benefits.[59] To stand against their attempts one must inquire, "How Shall We Interpret Separation
of Church and State in Education?"[60]

But this is only part of his thesis. His answer to the question
he raises is essentially negative: "separation" means that there
should be no contact between religion and government, and
thus that public education should be altogether secular. Thus
many others besides the Catholics fall under his displeasure.
"Breaches in the wall of separation" are caused not only by
those who clamor for free textbooks and bus rides for parochial
school children, but also by those who seek to associate religion
and public education in any way.

> . . . The influences which are bent upon transforming the present
> secular character of education in the United States are varied in-
> deed, ranging from individuals and groups who are determined to
> maintain the dominance of Protestants and Christians to those
> who would shape our educational systems in the image of a Catholic
> concept of the relation of church and state. Midway between these
> are those who wish to commit the schools to the teaching of a
> "common religious faith" in which Catholics and Protestants can
> share, even though "secularists" and the adherents of faiths out-
> side the Judaeo-Christian tradition are excluded thereby.[61]

Then does "separation" mean that religion must be completely banned? No, he says, adding in a burst of insight, "our fathers did not envisage banishing religion but merely sectarian teaching from education."[62] But this admission does not amount to much, for the joker is in the word "sectarian." Nearly everything is sectarian, and Thayer recognizes no middle ground between that extreme and secularism. Even teaching "a common core of religious faith" would be anathema, for "from the 'secularist's' point of view, . . . the common core of religion . . . is sectarian through and through."[63]

The secret of Thayer's opposition to any relationship between religion and government seems to lie therefore in his suspicion of religion. The plea that a "neutral attitude" may work negatively has no effect on him. He quotes Luther A. Weigle:

The ignoring of religion by the schools inevitably conveys to the children a negative suggestion. . . . It is natural for them to conclude that religion is negligible or unimportant, or irrelevant to the main business of life.[64]

Then Thayer comments,

One is tempted to ask, facetiously, whether the school's failure to include marble-playing in the curriculum leads to similar results.[65]

The answer of course is yes; when religion and marble-playing are both omitted, then both seem unimportant. The only difference may be, "facetiously," that when one of them is allowed on the school ground during recess; it may seem less unimportant than the other.

Now the school must be concerned with both morality and democracy. But here is the point at which Thayer shows most clearly his attitude toward religion. Morality does not depend on religion; "the common notion that religion underwrites morality . . . puts the cart before the horse."[66] Similarly, democracy depends not so much on "the concept of an 'ultimate reality to which supreme allegiance must be given'" as vice versa: "men . . . tend to endow the Deity . . . with the selfsame qualities they would translate into reality"—and he quotes Sidney Hook to justify the position![67] It is not surprising, therefore, to find that he concludes, "To perpetuate a secular emphasis . . . is indispensable for the continued growth of the democratic spirit."[68] And all this he rests on his rigid and disabling concept of "separation."

But men of a much different attitude toward religion are also found in the camp of the complete separationists. For instance, Conrad Henry Moehlman and Joseph Martin Dawson are staunch Baptists, and their restrictive concepts of church-state relations are, to their view, entirely consonant with their firm religious loyalties. In their latest volumes, Moehlman's *The Wall of Separation between Church and State* and Dawson's *America's Way in Church, State and Society*, they paint on a broader canvas than Thayer, for their concern is not alone with education. But their argument is the same, beginning with the danger of the Catholics' attitudes and actions—with which this writer agrees—and ending with the absoluteness of the Constitution's prohibition against any dealings between church and state— with which I cannot agree.

The Catholics are the chief problem, and in both books O'Neill comes in for special vilification.[69] But Dawson also holds up to scorn those Protestants who he thinks are playing the Catholic line; he quotes the same words of Weigle that

Thayer does, and with another quip—this one biting—likewise fails to answer him.[70] Both authors plow over the ground now familiar to us, and add no essential new material.

Butts's Errors

R. Freeman Butts, however, makes a substantial contribution to the discussion. That he is moved by fear of the Catholics is clear from the treatment of "The Struggle for Separation in Education in the Twentieth Century."[71] The whole volume, *The American Tradition in Religion and Education*, has the public school in mind as the battleground. But the battle is of broader concern, and it is the battle itself on which he focuses, the question as to how "separation" should be conceived. To understand it rightly calls for a knowledge of history. The value of Butts's book lies in its expert marshaling of much of the data that are relevant, and in the frankness, clarity, and even temper with which he states his own position.

This author has no special crow to pick with Butts's historical material. He treats, in greater detail than was possible in this volume, many of the matters referred to in previous chapters. To be sure he leans heavily on Jefferson and Madison, over-playing the part they took in the Federal development of the principle, and underplaying both the fact that they did not get all they desired in the way of limitations and the converse fact that they themselves approved some forms of governmental recognition and aid of religion, though not subsidization.[72] But it is not his history so much as it is his handling of it to which exception must be taken.

One is grateful that the basis of his interpretation is so clearly expressed. Recognizing that freedom of worship is interlocked with the relationship of church and state, he suggests that "four possible combinations" of "establishment" and "exercise" constitute "the choices before the American people":

(1) No establishment of religion; no free exercise of religion. . . .
(2) "Co-operation" between church and state with no religious freedom (single establishment; no free exercise of religion). . . .
(3) "Co-operation" between church and state with some freedom of religion. . . .
    (a) Single establishment with free exercise. . . .
    (b) Multiple establishment with free exercise. . . .
(4) Separation of church and state (no single or multiple establishment; complete freedom of religion). . . .[73]

Numbers (1), (2), and (3a), he recognizes, are not live options; "the genuine issue . . . for most Americans narrows down to a choice between (3b) or (4), to a choice between co-operation of the state with many churches or full separation of church and state."[74]

With this framework Butts undertakes to show that American history supports No. (4), and that all who believe in any kind or degree of "co-operation" are really in favor of some form of establishment. The fault is twofold: he omits from his classification an important position, namely, the one this book upholds; and because of this omission he herds all who disagree with him into his No. (3b).

As to the former, let it be phrased in consonance with the wording of his list; and since it is a position distinguishable from any he identifies, let it be called No. (5):

(5) No establishment; organic disconnection between church and state; sympathetic association between religion and government; full freedom of religion.

But even as with Butts's phraseology, so this is simply shorthand for the general position of this volume, which has already been described in previous chapters. It differs from No. (3b) in that it opposes the state's giving that kind of aid to one denomination, or to several, that would mean preferential treatment. That is, it stands firmly with Madison's famous "Remonstrance" against subsidization of one or many denominations as such. It has a disabling aspect. It differs from No. (4) in that it likewise opposes the notion that the state should have no contact with religion at all; that is, it stands equally firmly for the kind of association that characterizes the bulk of our national experience, an association with the organized religious life of the people on a nonsectarian basis. It has an enabling aspect.

The second error of Butts's interpretation of history is that, lacking No. (5) in his listing, he editorializes on his facts in such fashion as to make out that the choice is solely between Nos. (3b) and (4), an alternative the facts themselves do not support. Let us note a few examples. He quotes one of Madison's great speeches in Congress on the rights of minorities, and comments:

This argument surely means with respect to religion that, even if the majority of people hold to a certain religious belief, they have no right to violate the equal rights of conscience of the minority nor to use the power of government to support the majority's view. Even if the majority in America is Christian, the government may not be used to aid the Christian religion in violation of the conscience of non-Christian minorities. "Co-operation" of majority churches with the state is prohibited by the constitutional and civil rights of conscience.[75]

As between the first two and the third sentences, note the *non sequitur*. One might quibble that even the first two sentences are too sweeping; or does our religious liberty really mean that Utah can be polygamous if it jolly well wants to? But the third sentence is the serious slip of logic. The first two may not force us to the third; they may simply lead to the conclusion that that kind of co-operation that represents an invasion of minority rights is prohibited; other kinds may be not only permissible but desirable. Yet this safer conclusion is not really available to Butts as long as he does not recognize No. (5) in his listing.

Again, after reviewing the process by which the First Amendment was created, he interprets its meaning as follows:

> . . . This meant not only free exercise of religious worship based upon civil rights of conscience but also the prohibition of "co-operation" by the Federal Government with one or with many churches. "Co-operation" of church and state is just as inimical to the equal rights of conscience as free exercise is necessary to them. The generic term "religious freedom" requires "no establishment" as fully as it requires "free exercise."[76]

The third sentence, this time, is altogether sound, but Butts leaves the impression that if one believes the third he must accept the other two. He is seeking, once again, to equate co-operation with establishment; and he fails to distinguish between those kinds of co-operation that suggest "multiple establishment" and those that do not. Yet the history he cites supports No. (5) even more readily than No. (4).

One final illustration: quoting Jefferson and Madison at length, he concludes that their "allegiance to religious freedom and opposition to all forms of religious establishment never swerved."[77] Religious freedom, yes; but when one remembers that "establishment" is synonymous with "co-operation," then "all forms" is too strong. Both Madison and Jefferson were quite prepared to accept the co-operation of the churches in gaining religious freedom; in fact, as we have seen, if they had not it never would have been secured. Butts might complain that this is not what he meant; but if not, then he needs to

choose some better word than co-operation in order to summarize the things he deplores in No. (3b). He goes on:

That their ideas were not immediately and fully put everywhere
into practice is simply a result of the variety and diversity . . .
of American life.[78]

Not necessarily. It might be a result of America's truly possessing No. (5) as its philosophy instead of No. (4).

This failure to put strict interpretations of the American principle into practice bothers Butts now and then. He writes:

Despite the clarity of the principle of separation of church and
state as expressed in this authentic historical tradition, there have
been many practices continued which are in effect holdovers from
the pre-separation days of the seventeenth and eighteenth centuries. These practices include religious phraseology in several
state constitutions, the appointment and payment of chaplains for
Congress, for the armed forces, and for certain penal and chari-
table institutions, tax exemptions for religious institutions, religious
exercises at official ceremonies, and certain requirements for religious oaths and tests for officeholders of a few state governments.
The weight of evidence indicates that these practices are exceptions
to the principle of separation of church and state rather than practices which prove the principle of "co-operation" between church
and state. The principle is clearly "separation" and not "co-
operation."[79]

Several comments are in order. First, the list of practices is far
from exhaustive, as of course Butts would recognize. Second,
not all are "holdovers," for many of them have been instituted
in recent times; for example, not until the Eisenhower admin-
istration was a nonsectarian prayer chapel set aside for the use
of Congressmen. Most important, it is purely a personal opinion
that "the weight of evidence indicates that these practices are
exceptions to the principle of separation." It is true that they do

not "prove the principle of 'co-operation' " as he defines that principle; but it is not true that the choice must be made between those two.

The fact is, Butts's theory cannot incorporate these practices. But why leave them out? Why assign them arbitrarily to the category of "exceptions"? Why does Butts not do a better job of understanding the history, the total experience of Americans in church-state relations, that he so carefully resurrects?

Because his theory is too rigid, and thus unrealistic. One admires his recognition that No. (4) cannot take everything into account. One is glad to see further that he does not hesitate to follow through logically in line with the limitations of his hypothesis: he would rule out not only the various efforts to secure preferential treatment, but also such things as chaplains, all released-time programs, the nonsectarian teaching of religion, and all "indirect" as well as "direct aid."[80] But credit given for these insights, one is disappointed to find that he fails to read history in the light of a theory that can take into account all that he says plus the so-called "exceptions." The last sentence in the foregoing quotation is an editor's wish; to be accurate and all-embracing it should read, "The principle is clearly neither 'separation' nor 'co-operation' [as Butts defines those terms], but the two-fold standard of organic disconnection and sympathetic association of church and state." The "exceptions," too, are part of our American development; and our principle must be seen to be—for history and present practice show that it is—broad enough to include them.

Failure to Discriminate

The latest major protagonist for the complete-separation point of view is Leo Pfeffer, in his mammoth work *Church,*

State and Freedom. He was one of the counsel for the appellants in the Zorach case, and his writing reflects his agitation at the outcome. To escape needless repetition, let it simply be recorded that he covers nearly all the subjects heretofore noted and some others as well: Catholics and Mormons; Everson, McCollum, and Zorach; Jefferson, Madison, and O'Neill; and a complete catalogue of the various practices that seem to weaken the concept of "total and final separation."

Under his view of the American principle very little if any relationship between religion and government is possible. He finds highly questionable or throws out entirely not only preferential programs but also tax exemption, chaplains in Congress, religious holiday proclamations and celebrations, nearly all proposals for the teaching of religion, and "baccalaureate" services in public schools.[81] Though he notes "that Congress did not expressly bar nonpreferential aid to religion," he takes its failure to substitute a more unwieldy statement for the wording of the First Amendment as evidence "that it did not expressly limit the bar to preferential establishment."[82] He himself notes only a few allowable forms of association. Chaplains in the armed forces may be all right on military grounds.[83] "Objective teaching 'about' religion," though perhaps not "practicable," is "constitutionally permissible."[84] And religion that is "multisectarian and nondevotional" may be included in state universities.[85]

But even these bare permissions cause trouble for his theory. In his concluding "Ten Theses" his principle is monolithic: ". . . separation . . . was conceived to be as absolute as could be achieved, predicated as it was on the concept that religion is outside the jurisdiction of government."[86] There should be no "exceptions," and yet there are. What can be done about them?

Since man is imperfect, and does not lose all his imperfections when he enters the service of church or state, there have been deviations from the principle. Religious freedom has on occasions been interfered with, and the separation of church and state has on occasions been impaired. Those impairments have incorrectly been urged as evidence that it was not the intent of the framers of the First Amendment that the principle be absolute and the separation complete.[87]

But why say "incorrectly"? Not because the facts permit only that one interpretation of the instances of "nonpreferential aid"; rather simply because his theory is too rigid to take them into account in any other way.

This is the general fault of all the writers we have been considering. It is a basic failure to discriminate. All honor to them for their pointing out the danger of giving special aid to some groups, their alertness in defense of the restrictive aspect of our American principle. But they need to go one step further: they need to see there is a permissive aspect as well. They need to read the founding fathers without the glasses of their own theory. For the founding fathers, together with the whole American experience, support their narrow interpretation only when they are read through a narrow lens.

Sometimes the suggestion is heard—though I have seldom seen it in print—that those of us who take a broad position are lenient toward the Catholics. But the strange thing is that the position of the complete separationists may involve more bending to Catholic pressure. They are so eager to defeat the desires of one religious group that they are willing to abandon religion completely, as far as its relation with government is concerned. But this is as distressing as it is unnecessary. We need not criticize some program merely because the Catholics want it; we need not fail to support some measure simply because the Catholics support it. Discrimination, on the basis of a principle that calls for discrimination, is the better way.

Let me say, once again, that I oppose every effort of the Catholics to seize special advantage—textbooks here and bus rides there and representation at the Vatican yonder—but I deplore the idea of some of my good friends, "Protestants and Other Americans . . . ," that the only sound ground for opposition is a theory of rigid church-state separation that neither history upholds nor present practice supports. In the principle as it actually was and is we have all the protection we need, if we will use it intelligently and sensitively. Let us not allow freedom to become expediency; let us not maul our unique American machinery simply to dispel the Catholic danger.

Via Media

This, then, is our conclusion for these last two chapters: The establishment of religious freedom was largely a Protestant achievement; but, though many of the leaders understood what was being done, it was partly unintentional for the mass of effective followers. The result was not serious for two of the aspects of religious liberty, freedom to worship and a recognition of the supremacy of conscience; but the third, the relationship of church and state, was often misunderstood, even by the Supreme Court of the United States. Consequently attempts are being made to take advantage of this misunderstanding.

But if we need not go so far as to say "a plague o' both your houses," we may at least avoid the inviting ditches on each side by steering a straight path of principle down the middle way, the American Way. This means our continually calling to mind both aspects of this relationship, the restrictive one of organic disconnection and the permissive one of impartial association, in refutation of any who would emphasize either at the expense of the other. By no means does such a principle solve all our problems, for we shall be constantly perplexed by the application of the principle in marginal situations. But the puzzlement should be on matters of application, not on the principle as well. If we cannot please everybody, we ought at least to narrow the nature and area of our present displeasure.

There are bright rays of hope. A host of competent scholars are urging discrimination in the understanding and application of the principle. In this company are such men as M. Searle Bates, William Adams Brown, Edward S. Corwin, Evarts B. Greene, William E. Hocking, F. Ernest Johnson, James A. Pike, Liston Pope, Anson Phelps Stokes, Arthur E. Sutherland, William Warren Sweet, Henry P. Van Dusen, and Luther A. Weigle.[88] Differing among themselves on points of practice, they affirm the twofold character of the concept, that it means the absence of organic tie and the presence of nonsectarian support.

And—perhaps the most promising ray of all—the Supreme Court is now pointing in this direction. Unlike the opinions in the Everson and McCollum cases, Justice Douglas' majority opinion in *Zorach v. Clauson* tries to distinguish between the negative and positive aspects of American church-state relationships, and to put the Court's seal of approval on both. He writes:

There cannot be the slightest doubt that the First Amendment reflects the philosophy that Church and State should be separated. And so far as interference with the "'free exercise" of religion and an "establishment" of religion are concerned, the separation must be complete and unequivocal. The First Amendment, however, does not say that in every and all respects there shall be a separation of Church and State. Rather, it studiously defines the manner, the specific ways, in which there shall be no concert or union or dependency one on the other. That is the common sense of the matter. Otherwise the state and religion would be aliens to each other—hostile, suspicious, and even unfriendly.[89]

Then he reviews a variety of ways in which state and church associate, and continues:

We are a religious people whose institutions presuppose a Supreme Being. . . . When the state encourages religious instruction or co-operates with religious authorities . . . , it follows the best of our traditions. For it then respects the religious nature of our people and accommodates the public service to their spiritual needs. To hold that it may not would be to find in the Constitution a requirement that the government show a callous indifference to religious groups. That would be preferring those who believe in no religion over those who do believe. . . . We find no constitutional requirement which makes it necessary for government to be hostile to religion and to throw its weight against efforts to widen the effective scope of religious influence.[90]

Douglas still did not believe that the McCollum precedent was changed, and Jackson charged the majority with quibbling. Thus the Zorach case is hardly conclusive, but it does take a step toward a sound interpretation of the principle. Conscious of this step, Douglas recognizes further that it is not rigid "separation" that automatically prejudges such an issue as was before the Court, but that the question is in the area of the application of a more flexible relationship. He correctly concludes, "The problem, like many problems in constitutional law, is one of degree."[91] Perhaps we are outgrowing our misunderstanding. Perhaps we shall yet come to appreciate the American development of religious freedom in all its aspects.

CHAPTER VII

"Let Freedom Ring"

Where We Stand

MANY years ago Stephen Decatur offered his notorious toast, "Our country! In her intercourse with foreign nations, may she always be in the right; but our country, right or wrong!"

It does not require any argument for us to know that we who own to some religious faith, Christians and Jews alike, cannot accept such a statement. We call it false patriotism, for the religious man is loyal, first of all, to the right as God gives him to see it. He condemns the wrong, even if that wrong is adopted as part of his nation's policy. To uphold the right and to condemn the wrong are assertions of his freedom. But they are something more important than that: they constitute a reminder of the religious nature of freedom itself. We have noted earlier that the dimensions of freedom are rooted in a religious understanding of the nature of man and of the universe. To those who are aware of this foundation, freedom is therefore a form of obedience, a freely assumed submission to the character of Reality.[1] Freedom is not whim; it is not submission to one's self, and consequent self-assertion. Rather, it is compliance with the will of God—or with what one substitutes for God—a compliance that forces the individual to assert something he sees as greater than self. Thus for those for whom the nation is God, Decatur's toast may serve to summarize all the freedom they know; but for those who take seriously the ancient command, "Thou shalt have no other gods before me," Decatur's dictum is damnable.

To the Christian this point of view is all clear enough and would not call for special mention, were it not for another attitude, closely related to that of Decatur, which is common in our country. Those who hold this position seek to divide the spiritual and the temporal into completely separate realms. They admit freely that in the spiritual realm we as Christians must proclaim the right and oppose the wrong. But they contend that as Christians we have no business in passing moral judgment upon political matters, for whether we do so as individuals or as groups, that is an invasion of the temporal by the spiritual.[2]

This aberration is well illustrated by a statement of Congressman Tinkham of Massachusetts in 1924. Opposing a resolution brought by the former Federal Council of Churches concerning an immigration law then pending before Congress, he said:

It is one of the fundamental principles of the American Government . . . that there shall be in the United States complete separation of the church and the state as religious and political entities, and that there shall be no interference one with the other. The action of certain churches, of certain denominations . . . in passing resolutions in relation to legislation of a secular character . . . is indefensible. It is my settled opinion that some of the great lawlessness and actual crime in this country today is directly caused by the loss of respect for the church and its teachings on the part of the people, because churches abandoning spiritual affairs and direction have become quasi-political institutions.[3]

Tinkham's notion of the "complete separation of the church and the state" is, as we have already seen, unhistorical and false. It was never intended that "separation" should mean "that there shall be no interference one with the other," in the sense that religious groups would be prevented from giving their testimony on affairs of state; on the contrary, its very establishment was an illustration of the exercise of this right by such groups. But the churches' answer to Tinkham went even more to the heart of the matter. The petitioning group stated, "The Federal Council does not consider any question involving principles of right and justice as being secular."[4]

Here we become concerned not only with the religious nature of freedom but also with its subsidiary, the nature of religious freedom as the central element among all the rest of our liberties. When we speak of "freedom's holy light" we properly have both of these subjects in mind, and when we join in singing, "From every mountain side let freedom ring," we refer both to freedom in general and religious freedom, its focus, in particular. Clergy and laity alike must be concerned with religion in all its aspects, and thus with politics as one area of living in which religion inevitably enters. This is the meaning of the Federal Council's rejoinder.

The major marks of our liberty, therefore, have a religious base. Freedom of expression, of action, and of thought, reliance on consent, protection for dissent, and concern for the general welfare—all six of these are involved in, and receive their highest sanction from, religious freedom. That liberty itself, consisting of freedom to worship, the supremacy of conscience, and the "benevolent separation" of church and state, calls for continuous proclamation and the use of all the other so-called "secular" liberties in its enunciation. We have noted that the religious freedom that the Hebrew-Christian ethic desires is in remarkable measure the kind that Americans possess, in spite of the fact that along the way of its development there have been compromise, misunderstanding, and expediency. Yet if we are alert to the attempted dilutions of our religious liberty, we ought to be able to withstand from whatever direction the onslaughts of those who would take advantage of the misunderstandings still among us.

We ought to be able; and we must. If we see our loyalty to freedom as an expression of our religious faith, we have a much greater task than merely the defense and enhancement of religious liberty. We have more crucial business than, on the one hand, building roadblocks against the Catholics, or, on the other, escaping the dead ends to which those whom the Catholics have outmaneuvered would lead us. Both are important; but neither today can approach the potential significance of our speaking out, in the name of our faith, for the general freedom that America represents in the world.

We are prepared to join glad hands with secularists of all sorts who are willing to take brave part in the battle, but we have no right to rely solely on them. They do not have as much at stake. Only those who confess to the religious nature of freedom, and thus to the centrality of religious freedom, can view the present imperative as God's absolute. "Where the spirit of the Lord is, there is liberty." The character of our religious freedom gives us the right to work for its enhancement. Thus we who hear the voice of God to that effect should lead the way.

Problems of Declaration

Yet declaring our faith in freedom is not without its problems. Let us consider four cautions that need to be taken into account. The first two have to do with realizations affecting us as citizens, whatever our church affiliation or lack of it; the latter two have peculiar reference to loyal churchmen of all denominations.

First, it must never be forgotten that freedom entails adjustment.[5] Freedom calls for the assertion of the rights of others as well as of our own. More, it calls for the recognition of responsibilities as well as of rights. In a complex society such as ours, the impact of persons on each other, all of whom possess this kind of freedom, brings about a process of give and take, a large-scale and never-ending accommodation among the liberties of all. We need not retreat to the point of saying that therefore genuine freedom is realized only within us, for "stone walls do" still "a prison make, and iron bars a cage"; but we do need to realize that liberty properly eventuates for the individual in discipline, and for society in adaptability. The cry for freedom is not swashbuckling bravado; it is the tempered testament of our desire to live with others in peace and good will, no matter what the differences among us, to live and let live.

Second, the right and the duty to make this testament in every area of man's common life does not bestow on us the right to adopt the role of the expert in solving the problems of every area.[6] Church groups are not the only ones to need this advice, but church groups find the temptation particularly difficult to avoid. Freedom is a quality that characterizes the relationships among men; it is not a specific formula for ordering the details of those relationships. The protagonist for the spirit of freedom may call attention to its absence in one situation or may strive for its presence in another, but in each instance he will need the help of the competent specialist when ways and means are to be discussed. Thus citizens who speak for freedom—churchmen in solemn assembly very much included—must exercise great care in their declarations, lest they weaken their case by trying to play the part, say, of the professional politician, or the economist, or the expert in labor relations or international affairs.

Third, religious proponents of freedom face a special obstacle in the divisiveness of organized religion. That we in America fall into the three major categories of Catholic, Protestant, and Jew is only the beginning of the difficulty. We Protestants put up with a special scandal: the latest religious census indicates that there are over three hundred distinct groupings among us. The point is not that for this reason religion's testimony actually is less effective than it should be, though that point is thoroughly sound. Rather, the recognition of the moment is that this ought to be the case; that is, that this divisiveness ought to serve as a reminder to any one denomination, or even to any present combination among them, that none should take to itself the pretense of speaking for all. We Methodists, or we Protestants, or we Christians, may feel that we "are the people; and wisdom will die with" us. But the overwhelming fact of religious variance in America suggests that we take the precaution of not pontificating.

The fourth problem is closely related to the third. Our American principle of religious liberty is clear that the state may not indulge in sectarianism; but our American practice does not furnish us with sufficiently clear guidance as to what sectarianism is.[7] Thus, strangely, the uncertainty leaves the way open for both extremes of the present argument to seek advantages. As we noted in the preceding chapter, the Catholic would have us believe that his desires are not sectarian, and the anti-Catholic would try to convince us that not merely the Catholic proposals but any and all relations between religion and government are sectarian. One answer, which we have already noted, is that we need to make plain, on the one hand, that the Catholic way in church-state relations, in spite of their protests to the contrary, is the sectarian way; and on the other hand, that the complete separationists escape sectarianism only to fall into that other attitude that the American principle also eschews, namely, secularism, a kind of unconcerned "neutrality" that is the sectarianism of irreligion.

But another answer has to do not only with the recognition that both sectarianism and secularism are alike dangerous, but also with the admission that we need to exercise more discrimination than we have thus far sometimes shown in defining and then refraining from sectarianism. To be sure, the determination will not be easy, and it will probably differ from time to time and place to place. For example, some states prohibit the reading of the King James Version of the Bible in the public schools, on the grounds that it is a sectarian act; while other states allow the practice, and still others actually require it to be read.[8]

One might maintain that all that this diversity shows is that we do not know what sectarianism is; but one might with equal justice contend that each practice might be permissible for the locality in question, and that the diversity simply demonstrates that sectarianism is no absolute that applies to all places alike. But whichever way we happen to react to that particular problem, we can safely conclude from it that the definition of sectarianism is sufficiently difficult to constitute a warning to us. Men of religious faith speak best on behalf of freedom when they are alert to their own diversity that rules out both dogmatism and partisanship.

The Threat to Freedom

Taking these cautions into account, let us examine the threats to our freedom, and thus the subjects on which lovers of liberty must be prepared to express themselves. It is customary to group these threats into two great categories, and to give them directional designation, the Far Left and the Far Right. Thus our terminology leaves the impression that they are complete opposites, and that each is the only sure antithesis to the other.

On analysis, however, we discover that they are brothers under the skin. Though there are, of course, critical differences between them, the threat they pose to freedom is essentially the same—the menace of the authoritarian mind. Each represents a party line of faith and practice. Their confessed aims and purposes may be poles apart, but their attitudes toward their aims are identical. Both to the Far Left and the Far Right its own position is the ultimate truth, and all others are in grievous error.

The Far Left manifestation of the authoritarian mind is, of

course, communism. It usually exists in a society of its own construction, and thus its authoritarian impulses are not subject to any limitations. When it invades various types of free societies, it is called on to make some adjustments to the nature of freedom, including the need to forego the imposition of its doctrine on all alike. But there are sufficient places on the earth's surface where it now has the upper hand for us to see clearly the intransigence of its position.

If our subject were the challenge to freedom in the rest of the world we should need to devote large space to communism. But we Americans are so nearly of one accord on this matter that short shrift can be given to the threat it represents. This is possible not only because we are of one mind but also because it is of such small proportions. To recognize as much is not to condone those cases in which it has been ignored or, worse, palliated, in government, church, or anywhere else. But it is to say that, though communism is dangerous wherever it exists, it is not widespread in either numbers or influence. The important thing is that communism is simply not a live option for Americans; we want no part of it.

Yet, though communism holds no attraction for us, it may be useful briefly to note its characteristic ways of behavior. Four statements will suffice. First, communism cuts its supporters off from all the rest of mankind, for it sees all else as in opposition to it. Second, any deviation from strict party doctrine is interpreted as disloyalty; no degree of dissent is countenanced. Third, communism is cynical toward truth; the facts are bent to fit the case. And finally, the end justifies the means; and anything goes. We need not belabor the uncompromising opposition that freedom, particularly religious freedom, must furnish to such a system; all that has been said about the nature of freedom stands in striking contrast to communist attitudes and practices.

The Far Right, on its own premises, is not as fortunate as the Far Left. Because it now exists largely within the bounds of free societies, it is, paradoxically, less free to assert its full character. Germany, Italy, and Japan, those three nations in which it rose to its frankest expression, were defeated—though we should not forget that Franco and Péron still rule. But in the main the Far Right has to temporize with its protector and antagonist, freedom.

Consequently, in any free society the Far Right may not appear as in such bitter opposition to liberty as the Far Left. Yet because it is forced to go through the motions of democracy, it may thereby represent, in any particular situation, a greater peril than its leftist colleague. Its peril consists in the fact that, though it may become tinged with democracy, it may on the contrary succeed in infecting freedom itself. That is, free men may not as rapidly recognize the blandishments of the Far Right as they do those of the Far Left; for the Far Right, like the Far Left when it can, uses the instruments of liberty to effect its own illiberal ends.

This suggests a further resemblance between the two. Both extremes flaunt the words of freedom while they flout their meanings. If liberty were merely a matter of language, there would be no differences among us at home or abroad. We all say that we love liberty—which is an unconscious tribute to its abiding power. There is not a nation, nor hardly a segment of any people, who own to any opposite loyalty. Freedom's star is so bright that Far Right and Far Left alike must hitch their verbal wagons to it. But the tribute is discomfiting; it means we must look beyond protestation to performance.

In respect to the Far Right the task is not easy, for its manifestation of the authoritarian mind is more complex. Unlike the Far Left, no one word can summarize it, for it shows itself in various guises and gets called by diverse names. In politics it has been called fascism, Nazism, and totalitarianism, and lately its disciples in this country have been labeled "reactionaries." In business and industry it has been termed "rugged individualism," and its supporters "economic royalists." Two words of general application have recently become current, one self-inflicted and one the creation of the opposition. The self-styled title is "anti-communism," which is hardly satisfactory because of its implication that all others are somehow in the camp of the enemy. The opprobrious term is "McCarthyism," which probably gives the Senator too much credit and yet limits the scope of the disease. No one of these nor any other one word serves our purpose of summary delineation.

Moreover, to be descriptive of the Far Right as it shows itself in this country today calls for mention of the emotions of its adherents. Back when "rugged individualism" was in its heyday, its practitioners were supremely confident, scornful of any opposition, and sometimes pleasantly paternalistic. But times have changed; and those who now represent the Far Right are more likely to be characterized by frustration, anger, and fear. They are as a rule highly protective of their own interests and highly punitive against those whom they dislike. They are basically insecure; far from feeling any longer that the world is their oyster, they are liable to believe that things are topsy-turvy, the times are out of joint, and subversion is everywhere. Hate and distrust are their portion, and hysteria not seldom their fate.

In two quite common modes of behavior they take a value in which freedom believes and exaggerate it to the point of distortion. The first is seen in their attitude toward their country; the virtue is patriotism, and the exaggeration is jingoism. Now we have long had this superpatriotism with us; after all, Stephen Decatur was a hero of the War of 1812 and earlier. But the present flag-waving has a new intensity, and in certain areas a blatant regionalism accompanies it. The other position is "individualism"—though now with the "rugged" omitted. The value is the liberty of the individual to the full extent consonant with the like liberty of his fellows; the exaggeration is the philosophy of paddle-your-own-canoe, let-the-rest-of-the-world-go-by, and the-devil-take-the-hindmost.

More often, however, such people stand squarely against the values that freedom upholds, and many of their campaigns begin with the prefix "anti-." This is not the place for a full examination of their negativism, anger and fear, and in any event America is now sufficiently familiar with their techniques. Four summary statements may suffice. First, they show a tendency to draw a strict dividing line between their own small group on the one hand and all the rest of us on the other. Second, any deviation from the doctrine of the Far Right is looked upon as disloyalty, even "treason." In the third place, the strategy of name-calling in which they are adept has the effect of blurring the distinction between those who are willing to rest their case on the facts and those who are not; and truth gets lost in the shuffle. And finally, they show, as all this suggests, an insensitivity to method; the goal is the only concern, and any means of arriving at it is justifiable.[9]

Note the frightening identity between these four character-istic ways of behavior and those of the communists suggested above. It is, in fact, incorrect to speak of the Far Right and the Far Left as if there were two opponents of freedom, at least as to method. For the two are one, authoritarianism; and author-itarianism is the antithesis of freedom. Thus freedom disavows both—religious freedom especially. For freedom is a method as well as a content—again religious freedom especially. And freedom deplores the authoritarian methods of the Far Right for the same reasons as it does those of the Far Left.[10]

Freedom's Affirmations

Yet freedom is much more an affirmative concept than a negative one. Those who love liberty have more important business than simply the exposure of the distortions and false-hoods of communists and "anti-communists." Defenses against them often seem a waste of time. Take Bishop Oxnam for an example. In exchange for the careful and courageous way in which he refuted the calculated, unfactful charges of the Velde Committee against him, he received for his pains the effrontery of a "clearance."[11] Perhaps David Lilienthal did not achieve much more; in his ordeal before Senator McKellar his famous extemporaneous statement of his faith in democracy seemed to move McKellar not at all.[12]

Yet such stands are not fruitless; their value consists in their speaking positively to an audience beyond the bounds of their immediate detractors to whom they have to speak defensively. Though the Velde Committee retracts and McKellar passes on, other committees and other Congressmen continue their work. Men of that stamp of mind seem to be beyond the possibility of conversion to the true meaning of freedom; and the good to be gained from inescapable dealings with them is a larger good, the ringing affirmations of liberty that give strength and conviction to the flabby-hearted rest of us.

Our major task therefore is to state our faith in freedom in positive terms. Here is where those who disagree with each other at various points along the route of liberty's delineation can close ranks on the essential issues. Even O'Neill and Blanshard, who fire prejudiced popguns at each other, man the cannon together.[13] The cannon is aimed at communist and "anti-communist" alike. But maybe the cannon is an unfortunate figure, for freedom, if it holds out little hope of their conversion, does not say, "Off with their heads!" Justice Holmes's well-known dissent in *United States v. Schwimmer*—especially now that that decision has been overruled in the Girouard case—is a reminder to lovers of liberty as well as to authoritarian minds:

If there is any principle of the Constitution that more imperatively calls for attachment than any other it is the principle of free thought—not free thought for those who agree with us but freedom for the thought that we hate.[14]

Freedom does not condone the methods of unfreedom; it says, "Expose," not "Expunge."[15]

And then liberty states its own case. That case is being brilliantly stated today, by hosts of competent men and women, on general questions and in particular issues.[16] All the aspects of freedom noted in Chapter I are expounded with conviction and stern winsomeness; and it remains to us here only to call

attention to those affirmations that, with special religious con-
notations and justifications, are of peculiar concern to religious
freedom in particular. Those who believe in the religious nature
of freedom, and accept the full-fledged nature of religious
freedom as general freedom's central element, will join with all
other lovers of liberty in affirming the usual catalogue of rights
and responsibilities, and then will emphasize some of them as
especially relevant for men of religious orientation. Even here
they are not alone; free men of secular disposition do, in fact,
subscribe to all that is about to be said. Effort is not being made
to draw a line of distinction between what secularists and religionists do or should uphold; rather, the point is simply that,
whatever else others may do, men of religious faith must proclaim certain positions because of that faith. And because freedom is what it is, all of us have a right to expect that men of
religious faith will possess an extra dynamic in asserting some of
its implications.

Four such emphases may be mentioned. First, we have a
right to expect that churchmen, clergy and laity alike, will
speak forthrightly on behalf of the development of a sense of
community in regional, national, and international affairs. It is
distressing, for example, to see some Americans succumb to the
current anti-U.N. sentiment, and that largely out of ignorance;
for surely those who oppose the United Nations in spite of the
facts are a minor portion of the total antagonism. It is especially distressing to find some sincere churchmen in that company; and almost equally deplorable to discover other churchmen who are afraid to speak in favor of the U.N., lest they be
subject to name-calling. The Hebrew-Christian tradition does
not necessitate ignoring or excusing the failures and weaknesses

of the United Nations; but it does suggest that efforts at a free association of all the peoples of the world are in line with both the premises of liberty and the demands of the Hebrew-Christian ethic. Whenever men of religious faith interpret our freedom to mean a sense of community, they are true both to their faith and to the nature of freedom.

In the second place, faith and freedom incorporate brotherhood; they demand that it be demanded and that its denials be denied. Here is one place where communism has the edge over its fellow of the Far Right, for communists prate and when it is to their advantage perform like brothers, whereas the angry home-grown authoritarians often lend themselves to various scapegoat mechanisms, such as anti-Negro, anti-Mexican, anti-Catholic sentiment, and the ancient Christian calumny, anti-Semitism. That freedom sits in judgment on such infamies is an old story; it should be an even older story for the Hebrew-Christian tradition. For religion places the love of neighbor next to the love of God; and all who treasure their religious heritage take their firm stand for brotherly behavior, with no limitations of race, class, creed, or station, as being part of the meaning of liberty.

Third, religionists must insist on the truth and on its free search. Time and again the Far Left and the Far Right torture the facts to fit their fancies. The communist strategy is well exposed, but its opposite partner often throws dust in American eyes. We had a name for it during the time of Hitler, the technique of the "Big Lie." Sometimes today it is known by another anti-, "anti-intellectualism." Whatever it is called, it is a disrespect for the truth, and by association, a sometimes violent attack on those institutions specially dedicated to a free search and a proclamation of the truth: schools, colleges, universities, and churches. Thus churchmen and educators often bear the brunt of this challenge to freedom, and often feel themselves to be under more serious fire than at any previous time in the history of the nation.

Yet it is not with negation that we are primarily concerned, for defensiveness alone will not repair the breach in the house of freedom. All lovers of liberty who recognize truth as man's truth will say their piece in its behalf; all believers in God who recognize truth as God's truth will speak out from special compulsion. Freedom and faith alike detest a lie, even when buttressed by a misunderstood Bible or clothed with a desecrated flag. For Bible and flag, each in its separate way, are monuments to the uninhibited search for truth, and those who believe in both will take their public stand that only truth can support freedom.

The fourth insistence must be on fair play. Hitting in the clinches or when a man is down takes many a strange form, and communists have unwittingly taught their tricks to their supposedly extreme opposites. Picking a word or an action out of context, determining guilt by association or even less, preventing a man from facing his accusers, bribing, needling, whispering—such methods undermine our freedom and, more, our whole moral fiber. Thus those who know that the maintenance of liberty stands on moral stamina, and moral stamina on religious faith, must be the first to enunciate the decent rules of the game and to abide by them.

These, then, are among the positive virtues of freedom that the man of religious faith will expound and seek to emulate: sense of community, brotherhood, respect for truth, and fair play. Taken together, they come close to being what the Christian means by love in human relationships. Freedom is not full-fledged Christian love, but it is at the gateway to love. Those who do not understand freedom will always charge those who do with being soft toward communism or authoritarianism of any kind. But one pays a price to be free; and the religious man knows the price—something akin to that of love. Freedom is of the order of softness that love is—the highest, hardest demand ever made on men.[17] Even though we were born free, we still must pay the price—to build an unshakable faith in all the dimensions of general freedom; to find their focus in the three major aspects of religious freedom, correctly conceived both as to the Hebrew-Christian desire and as to the American development; to speak out in accordance with both the religious nature of freedom and the nature of religious freedom, on all the issues of our time; and to live like free men.

When opposition comes the price may seem high. Yet it is never too high—never as great as the value of liberty. Literally, freedom is not price-less, but it is priceless, worthful beyond compare, the most precious of the distinctive American creations. If pride is ever pardonable, we find excuse for our delight in the possession of freedom to worship as each man sees fit, the recognition by government of the supremacy of conscience, and a type of relationship between church and state that provides for both organic disconnection and sympathetic association.

We have this treasure, and those of us of religious faith ought specially to treasure it. We have a chance for the application of the Hebrew-Christian ethic to problems of state, with the least amount of extraneous considerations since the days of early Christianity. Up to the time of Constantine the church spoke equivocally, because of the necessity of survival in an unfriendly regime. After the time of Constantine the church continued to speak equivocally, because of the need to maintain a preferential position. But America broke the pattern, for the individual and the group; and the nature of our religious freedom, which undergirds all our liberties, enables us to state our Christian case on its merits, undiluted by either favor or disfavor. Then let us give truth a chance, give conscience a voice, give God a hearing. If we believe in "freedom's holy light," then "let freedom ring," let that light shine!

Notes

Chapter 1.   "SWEET LAND OF LIBERTY"

[1] See Eduard Heimann, *Freedom and Order* (New York: Charles Scribner's Sons, 1947); Eivind Berggrav, *Man and State* (Philadelphia: Muhlenberg Press, 1951), Ch. 8; Reinhold Niebuhr, *The Children of Light and the Children of Darkness* (New York: Charles Scribner's Sons, 1944).

[2] See M. Searle Bates, *Religious Liberty: An Inquiry* (New York: International Missionary Council, 1945), Ch. 3, Sec. 4, Ch. 4, especially pp. 418-432; Anson Phelps Stokes, *Church and State in the United States* (New York: Harper & Brothers, 1950), Vol. III, Ch. 27; Barbara Ward, *Faith and Freedom* (New York: W. W. Norton, 1954), Ch. 20; Samuel E. Stumpf, *A Democratic Manifesto* (Nashville: Vanderbilt Univ. Press, 1954), especially Chs. 2, 5; James H. Nichols, *Democracy and the Churches* (Philadelphia: Westminster Press, 1951), Ch. 1; Elton Trueblood, *Declaration of Freedom* (New York: Harper & Brothers, 1955), Ch. 6; Helmut Kuhn, *Freedom Forgotten and Remembered* (Chapel Hill: Univ. of North Carolina Press, 1943), pp. 101-108, 250-255; Heimann, *op. cit.*, Part III; Berggrav, *op. cit.*, Chs. 4, 6.

[3] See Hoxie N. Fairchild, "Religious Faith and Loyalty," *New Republic* (October 11, 1954), pp. 11-13; William Lee Miller, "Religion, Politics and the Great Crusade," *Reporter*, IX (July 7, 1953), pp. 14-16, and "Piety Along the Potomac," *Reporter*, XI (August 17, 1954), pp. 25-28.

[4] Psalm 100:3. The Revised Standard Version has: "It is he that made us, and we are his."

[5] See Wilhelm Pauck, *The Heritage of the Reformation* (Boston: Beacon Press, 1950), pp. 212-227; Winfred Ernest Garrison, *A Protestant Manifesto* (Nashville: Abingdon-Cokesbury Press, 1952), pp. 190-200; Sanford H. Cobb, *The Rise of Religious Liberty in America* (New York: Macmillan, 1902), Ch. 2; Bates, *op. cit.*, Ch. 2; Stumpf, *op. cit.*, *passim*; Nichols, *op. cit.*, Ch. 1.

[6] Thomas Hobbes, *Leviathan* (London: J. M. Dent & Sons, 1931), p. 65.

[7] John Locke, *Of Civil Government* (London: J. M. Dent & Sons, 1924), Book II.

[8] See George Macaulay Trevelyan, *History of England* (London: Longmans, Green, 1933), pp. 375-377, 486-497, 506.

[9] See Clinton Rossiter, *Seedtime of the Republic* (New York: Harcourt, Brace, 1953); John M. Mecklin, *The Story of American Dissent* (New

York: Harcourt, Brace, 1934), pp. 290, 292, 298, 342; Stokes, *op. cit.*, *passim*; Bates, *op. cit.*, pp. 211-214; William Warren Sweet, "The American Colonial Environment and Religious Liberty," *Church History*, Vol. 4 (1935), pp. 43-56.

[10] See Evarts B. Greene, *Religion and the State* (New York: New York Univ. Press, 1941), Ch. 1; Cobb, *op. cit.*, Ch. 2; Stumpf, *op. cit.*, pp. 118-138; Nichols, *op. cit.*, Ch. 1; Bates, *op. cit.*, pp. 148-179, 349, 418-424; Ernst Troeltsch, *The Social Teaching of the Christian Churches* (New York: Macmillan, 1950), Vol. II, pp. 490-494.

[11] See John S. Marshall, *Hooker's Polity in Modern English* (Sewanee: Univ. of the South Press, 1948), pp. 1-17; and his "Richard Hooker and the Origins of American Constitutionalism," in Arthur L. Harding, *ed.*, *Origins of the Natural Law Tradition* (Dallas: Southern Methodist Univ. Press, 1954), pp. 48-68.

[12] John Milton, "The Tenure of Kings and Magistrates," in J. A. St. John, *ed.*, *The Prose Works of John Milton* (London: G. Bell & Sons, 1914), Vol. II, pp. 8-9.

[13] See John Locke, *Essay Concerning Human Understanding*, II, xxi, in Critical edition ed. Alexander Campbell Fraser (Oxford: Clarendon Press, 1894), Vol. I, pp. 308-380; also his *Reasonableness of Christianity*, in *The Works of John Locke*, Vol. III (London, 1777), pp. 2-272, and his *An Essay Concerning the True Original Extent and End of Civil Government* (New York: D. Appleton-Century, 1937), Chs. 2, 9. See also R. I. Aaron, *John Locke* (London: Oxford Univ. Press, 1937), pp. 269-271, 295-299; Roland H. Bainton, *The Travail of Religious Liberty* (Philadelphia: Westminster Press, 1951), pp. 236-252; Stokes, *op. cit.*, Vol. I, pp. 142-147.

[14] See *ibid.*, Vol. I, pp. 552-554; Vol. III, pp. 656-657, 702, 714-718; Rossiter, *op. cit.*, pp. 36-37; Ward, *op. cit.*, Ch. 20; Stumpf, *op. cit.*, *passim*; Bates, *op. cit.*, Ch. 3.

[15] See John S. Marshall, *op. cit.*; F. J. Shirley, *Richard Hooker and Contemporary Political Ideas* (London: S.P.C.K., 1949); Christopher Morris, *Political Thought in England: Tyndale to Hooker* (London: Oxford Univ. Press, 1953), pp. 172-198; Ralph Henry Gabriel, "The Enlightenment Tradition," in F. Ernest Johnson, *ed.*, *Wellsprings of the American Spirit* (New York: Harper & Brothers, 1948), pp. 39-47; Aaron, *op. cit.*; Stokes, *op. cit.*, Vol. I, pp. 140-147; Philo M. Buck, Jr., *Milton on Liberty* (Lincoln, Neb.: Univ. of Nebraska, 1925), University Studies, Vol. 25, no. 1.

Chapter II. FREEDOM TO WORSHIP

[1] See William A. Irwin, *The Old Testament: Keystone of Human Culture* (New York: Henry Schuman, 1952), pp. 100-101, 104-106, 206-212; R. B. Y. Scott, *The Relevance of the Prophets* (New York: Macmillan, 1947), pp. 196-210, 223-227; William Creighton Graham, *The*

Prophets and Israel's Culture (Chicago: Univ. of Chicago Press, 1934), pp. 87-96.

² See Thomas Walter Manson, *The Teaching of Jesus* (London: Cambridge Univ. Press, 1931), pp. 157-164; Maurice Goguel, *The Life of Jesus* (New York: Macmillan, 1933), pp. 553-586; B. Harvie Branscomb, *The Teachings of Jesus* (Nashville: Cokesbury Press, 1931,) pp. 364-374.

³ See C. H. Dodd, *Gospel and Law* (New York: Columbia Univ. Press, 1951); Manson, *op. cit.*; Goguel, *op. cit.*; Branscomb, *op. cit.*, pp. 357-374.

⁴ Galatians 5:1. See Edgar J. Goodspeed, *Paul* (Philadelphia: John C. Winston, 1947), pp. 106-112; Morton Scott Enslin, *The Ethics of Paul* (New York: Harper & Brothers, 1930), pp. 75, 85, 126, 242-254; *Interpreter's Bible* (Nashville: Abingdon-Cokesbury, 1953), Vol. X, pp. 544 ff.

⁵ See Troeltsch, *op. cit.*, Vol. I, pp. 69-89; Williston Walker, *A History of the Christian Church* (New York: Charles Scribner's Sons, 1921), pp. 28-32; Kenneth Scott Latourette, *A History of Christianity* (New York: Harper & Brothers, 1953), pp. 197-220; Cobb, *op. cit.*, Ch. 2; Bates, *op. cit.*, Ch. 2.

⁶ See references in fn. 2, Ch. 1, *supra;* Ilion T. Jones, *A Historical Approach to Evangelical Worship* (Nashville: Abingdon Press, 1954), pp. 283-301.

⁷ See Stokes, *op. cit.*, Vol. I, Ch. 3, Sec. 2 (1); Greene, *op. cit.*, pp. 37, 42, 43; Bates, *op. cit.*, pp. 180-183; Mecklin, *op. cit.*, Ch. 4; Cobb, *op. cit.*, pp. 67-70; William Warren Sweet, *Religion in Colonial America* (New York: Charles Scribner's Sons, 1942), pp. 88-95.

⁸ See Stokes, *op. cit.*, Vol. I, pp. 169-184; Greene, *op. cit.*, pp. 42-43; Bates, *op. cit.*, pp. 180, 353; Mecklin, *op. cit.*, Chs. 6, 7; Sweet, *op. cit.*, pp. 131-138, 144-150.

⁹ See Bainton, *op. cit.*, pp. 213-218; Bates, *op. cit.*, pp. 155, 182; Stokes, *op. cit.*, Vol. I, pp. 159, 160, 177, 178, 180, 183, 184; Greene, *op. cit.*, pp. 43, 44, 49.

¹⁰ See Cobb, *op. cit.*, *passim;* Sweet, *op. cit.*, *passim;* Bates, *op. cit.*, pp. 179-186, 216; Greene, *op. cit.*, pp. 30, 31, 45, 64, 68; Stokes, *op. cit.*, Vol. I, pp. 152, 170, 854-859.

¹¹ See Bainton, *op. cit.*, Ch. 8; Rossiter, *op. cit.*, Ch. 7; Stokes, *op. cit.*, Vol. I, pp. 194-202; Greene, *op. cit.*, pp. 47-51; Cobb, *op. cit.*, pp. 423-436.

¹² Quoted in Stokes, *op. cit.*, Vol. I, p. 199. For John Clarke's influence, see *ibid.*, pp. 202-205.

¹³ See Rossiter, *op. cit.*, p. 46; Cobb, *op. cit.*, pp. 437-438; Greene, *op. cit.*, p. 51; Stokes, *op. cit.*, Vol. I, pp. 857, 859.

¹⁴ See Sweet, *op. cit.*, pp. 168-181; Stokes, *op. cit.*, Vol. I, pp. 189-194; Greene, *op. cit.*, pp. 53-56; Cobb, *op. cit.*, pp. 362 ff.

¹⁵ See Stokes, *op. cit.*, Vol. I, p. 194; Cobb, *op. cit.*, pp. 387 ff.; Sweet, *op. cit.*, pp. 181-183; Bates, *op. cit.*, pp. 184, 211.

¹⁶ See Greene, *op. cit.*, pp. 56-59; Stokes, *op. cit.*, Vol. I, pp. 206-208; Cobb, *op. cit.*, pp. 440-452; Sweet, *op. cit.*, pp. 158-163.

¹⁷ Quoted in Stokes, *op. cit.*, Vol. I, p. 206.

[18] See Cobb, *op. cit.*, pp. 444-451; Stokes, *op. cit.*, Vol. I, p. 859; Bates, *op. cit.*, p. 210; Greene, *op. cit.*, p. 58.

[19] See Rossiter, *op. cit.*, Ch. 2; Cobb, *op. cit.*, *passim;* Stokes, *op. cit.*, Vol. I, p. 167, Ch. 3, Secs. 3, 4; Greene, Chs. 3, 4; Bates, *op. cit.*, pp. 210-218.

[20] See Rossiter, *op. cit.*, Part I; Stokes, *op. cit.*, Vol. I, Ch. 3, Sec. 4 (1) (2) (6) (7), Ch. 4, Secs. 2, 3, 7; Greene, *op. cit.*, Chs. 3, 4.

[21] See Cobb, *op. cit.*, p. 482; Rossiter, *op. cit.*, p. 46; Greene, *op. cit.*, pp. 69, 81; Bates, *op. cit.*, p. 216.

[22] For the work of Davies, etc., see Stokes, *op. cit.*, Vol. I, pp. 208-216, 366-379; for the story of the Virginia development, see *ibid.*, Ch. 5, Sec. 3; Greene, *op. cit.*, pp. 78, 85-88; Cobb, *op. cit.*, pp. 74-115, 490-499.

[23] Quoted in *ibid.*, p. 491.

[24] *Ibid.*, p. 492.

[25] Art. XVI, The Bill of Rights of Virginia, 1776, quoted in *ibid.*, pp. 491-492. See a slightly different version quoted in Rossiter, *op. cit.*, pp. 400-401.

[26] See Stokes, *op. cit.*, Vol. I, Ch. 5, Secs. 4, 5, 8; Cobb, *op. cit.*, Ch. 9.

[27] Art. VI, par. 3, states: " . . . no religious Test shall ever be required as a Qualification to any Office or public Trust under the United States." For the story of the Federal Constitution debates and actions on religious freedom, see Stokes, *op. cit.*, Vol. I, pp. 519-537.

[28] See *ibid.*, Vol. I, pp. 537-549, 553, 559, 576, 612 ff.; Vol. III, p. 634.

[29] *Marbury v. Madison*, 1 Cranch 137.

[30] See Stokes, *op. cit.*, Vol. I, pp. 570-573.

[31] See *Cantwell v. Connecticut*, 310 U.S. 296; *Murdock v. Pennsylvania*, 319 U.S. 105; *West Virginia State Board of Education v. Barnette*, 319 U.S. 624; Stokes, *op. cit.*, Vol. I, pp. 575-591; William George Torpey, *Judicial Doctrines of Religious Rights in America* (Chapel Hill: Univ. of North Carolina Press, 1948), pp. 28-31.

[32] Stokes, *op. cit.*, Vol. I, p. 556. See also *ibid.*, Vol. III, Ch. 24; R. Kemp Morton, *God in the Constitution* (Nashville: Cokesbury Press, 1933), pp. 58 ff., 152 ff.; William Adams Brown, *Church and State in Contemporary America* (New York: Charles Scribner's Sons, 1936), pp. 104-105; Cobb, *op. cit.*, pp. 524-527.

Chapter III.   THE SUPREMACY OF CONSCIENCE

[1] See Reinhold Niebuhr, *Moral Man and Immoral Society* (New York: Charles Scribner's Sons, 1948), pp. 96-97; Troeltsch, *op. cit.*, Vol II, pp. 491-494, 516 ff.; Cobb, *op. cit.*, pp. 45-46; Perry Miller, "The Contribution of the Protestant Churches to Religious Liberty in Colonial America," *Church History*, Vol. 4 (1935), pp. 57-66.

[2] See *Interpreter's Bible*, Vol. 7, pp. 882-883; Goguel, *op. cit.*, pp. 492-495; Branscomb, *op. cit.*, pp. 357-374.

[3] See Reinhold Niebuhr, "The Ethic of Jesus and the Social Problem,"

Religion in Life, Vol. I, No. 2 (Spring, 1932), p. 199; Goguel, *op. cit.;* Branscomb, *op. cit.;* Manson, *op. cit.*

[4] Romans 13:1, Revised Standard Version.

[5] See Emil Brunner, *The Divine Imperative* (Philadelphia: Westminster Press, 1947), pp. 460-462, 473-474; William A. Spurrier, *Power for Action* (New York: Charles Scribner's Sons, 1948), pp. 43-56.

[6] See William Ernest Hocking, *Man and the State* (New Haven: Yale Univ. Press, 1926), Ch. 28; Paul Ramsey, *Basic Christian Ethics* (New York: Charles Scribner's Sons, 1951), p. 357; Brunner, *op. cit.,* pp. 473-474; Berggrav, *op. cit.,* Ch. 15.

[7] See Stokes, *op. cit.,* Vol. II, pp. 275-285; Kimball Young, *Isn't One Wife Enough?* (New York: Henry Holt, 1954).

[8] *Reynolds v. United States,* 98 U.S. 145; see also *Miles v. United States,* 103 U.S. 304, and *Territory of Idaho v. Evans,* 2 Idaho 651.

[9] *Davis v. Beason,* 133 U.S. 333. See Mark DeWolfe Howe, *Cases in Church and State in the United States* (Cambridge: Harvard Univ. Press, 1952), pp. 237-242.

[10] *Late Corporation of the Church of Jesus Christ of Latter-Day Saints v. United States,* 136 U.S. 1.

[11] *People v. Ruggles,* 8 Johns 289.

[12] *Idem.*

[13] *Idem.*

[14] *Idem.*

[15] See, for example, *People v. Most,* 171 N.Y. 423; *Commonwealth v. Kneeland,* 20 Pick. 206; *State v. Mockus,* 120 Me. 84; *Lindenmuller v. People,* 33 Barb. 548; *State v. Chandler,* 2 Harr. 553; *Zeissweiss v. James,* 63 Penn. St. 465; *Updegraph v. Commonwealth,* 11 S. & R. 394; *City Council v. Benjamin,* 2 Strob. 508; *Church of the Holy Trinity v. United States,* 143 U.S. 457. See also Morton, *op. cit.,* Ch. 3.

[16] *Updegraph v. Commonwealth, op. cit.*

[17] *Idem.*

[18] See, for example, *People v. Most, op. cit.; State v. Mockus, op. cit.; Pirkey Bros. v. Commonwealth,* 134 Va. 713.

[19] See, for example, *State v. Chandler, op. cit.; Lindenmuller v. People, op. cit.; State v. Mockus, op. cit.; Pirkey Bros. v. Commonwealth, op. cit.* See also William Bruce Hoff, "Religious Freedom Under Our Constitutions," *West Virginia Law Quarterly,* XXXI (December, 1924); Torpey, *op. cit.,* pp. 31-34. If Christianity as a religion, rather than merely that part of Christianity recognized as the Christian ethic, were held to be part of the common law, *Runkel v. Winemiller,* Maryland, 1799, rather than *People v. Ruggles,* would probably have become the leading authority, for this case states much more categorically that "the Christian religion is the established religion"; see *Runkel v. Winemiller,* 4 Harr. & McH. 429.

[20] *State v. Chandler, op. cit.*

[21] See Ramsey, *op. cit.,* Chs. 1, 2; Brunner, *op. cit.,* pp. 82 ff.; Reinhold

Niebuhr, *An Interpretation of Christian Ethics* (New York: Harper & Brothers, 1935), pp. 3-34.

[22] The Constitution of Utah, Article III; see Charles Kettleborough, *The State Constitutions* (Indianapolis: B. F. Bowen, 1918).

[23] See Stokes, *op. cit.*, Vol. III, pp. 270-273; Greene, *op. cit.*, pp. 142-145; *Christian Century*, Vol. 46 (July 10, 1929), pp. 888-889; Vol. 47 (July 9, 1930), p. 859; Vol. 47 (Aug. 6, 1930), pp. 961-963.

[24] *United States v. Macintosh*, 283 U.S. 605; *United States v. Schwimmer*, 279 U.S. 644.

[25] *United States v. Macintosh, op. cit.*

[26] See Brown, *op. cit.*, pp. 20, 28, 156; Stokes, *op. cit.*, Vol. III, pp. 273-274; *Christian Century*, Vol. 48, June 3, 10, 24, July 1, 22, Sept. 30, Oct. 21, Nov. 11, 1931.

[27] *Girouard v. United States*, 328 U.S. 61.

[28] *Idem.; United States v. Bland*, 283 U.S. 636.

[29] *United States v. Macintosh, op. cit.*

[30] *Girouard v. United States, op. cit.*

[31] *Idem.*

[32] *Idem.*

[33] Bates, *op. cit.*, p. 90.

[34] Stokes, *op. cit.*, Vol. III, pp. 269-274.

[35] Bates, *op. cit.*, p. 93; Stokes, *op. cit.*, Vol. II, pp. 600-616; Vol. III, pp. 220-224.

[36] *Minersville School District v. Gobitis*, 310 U.S. 586.

[37] *Idem.*

[38] *West Virginia State Board of Education v. Barnette, op. cit.*

[39] *Idem.*

[40] *Girouard v. United States, op. cit.*

[41] See *United States v. Kauten*, 133 Fed. 2 703; Stokes, *op. cit.*, Vol. III, p. 303; Brunner, *op. cit.*, p. 473; Torpey, *op. cit.*, Ch. 2.

[42] See *Hamilton v. Regents of the Univ. of California*, 293 U.S. 245; Greene, *op. cit.*; p. 98; Brunner, *op. cit.*; p. 469; Ramsey, *op. cit.*; pp. 330-331; Torpey, *op. cit.*, pp. 43-46.

Chapter IV.   THE INDEPENDENCE OF CHURCH AND STATE

[1] See *infra*, pp. 119, 125. See also *Our Bishops Speak* (Milwaukee: Bruce Pub. Co., 1952), pp. 3-65; Joseph E. Cunneen, "Catholics and Education," in *Catholicism and America* (New York: Harcourt, Brace, 1953), pp. 143-163; Frederick G. Hochwalt, "A Catholic Educator's View," in F. Ernest Johnson, ed., *American Education and Religion* (New York: Harper & Brothers, 1952), pp. 61-76; John A. O'Brien, in *Christian Century*, Vol. 65, No. 20 (May 19, 1948), pp. 473-476; Stokes, *op. cit.*, Vol. II, pp. 393-394, 682; Vol. III, pp. 451-452, Ch. 23, Sec. 4(1), Ch. 25, Sec. 3(2); Nichols, *op. cit.*, Chs. 4, 6, 7, 9; George H. Dunne, *The Catholic Church and Politics: A Discussion on a Vital Issue* (Cambridge: Harvard Law

School Forum, 1950), pp. 29-30; John Tracy Ellis, "Church and State: An American Catholic Tradition," *Harper's*, Vol. 207, No. 1242 (November 1953), pp. 63-67.

[2] See *Five Great Encyclicals* (New York: Paulist Press, 1939), pp. 37-75 (Pius XI on Christian Education of Youth); Nichols, *op. cit.*, Chs. 4, 6, 7, 9; Stokes, *op. cit.*, Vol. III, pp. 16, 451, 454 ff.; Brown, *op. cit.*, Ch. 8; Bates, *op. cit.*, pp. 188-193, 324-330, 432-468; Christopher Dawson, *Religion and the Modern State* (New York: Sheed & Ward, 1937), Ch. 8.

[3] See *infra*, pp. 126-143. See also Nevin C. Harner, "A Protestant Educator's View," in *American Education and Religion, op. cit.*, pp. 83-84; F. Ernest Johnson, "Policies and Practices of American Public Schools in Respect to Religion," *Religion and Public Education, American Council on Education Studies*, IX, 22 (February, 1945); F. Ernest Johnson, "Religion and Public Education," *Current Religious Thought*, Vol. 10, No. 2 (February, 1950), pp. 23-28; Morton, *op. cit.*, pp. 58-69; Brown, *op. cit., passim.*

[4] *The Writings of Thomas Jefferson*, Monticello Edition (Washington: The Thomas Jefferson Memorial Association, 1904), Vol. 16, pp. 281-282.

[5] See *infra*, pp. 91-102.

[6] Scholars who take such a position know that history supports them; see *infra*, p. 144. Thus reference is made not to them but to the lay public who desire religion in the schools but are fearful that no legally permissible method is available. Illustrations of this unnecessary nervousness appear in the daily press and in school board discussions whenever the subject is broached in any community.

[7] See *infra*, pp. 126-143.

[8] See Harner, *op. cit.;* John C. Bennett, "Implications of the New Conception of 'Separation,'" *Christianity and Crisis*, Vol. 8, No. 12 (July 5, 1948), pp. 89-90; "Statement on Church and State," *ibid.*, p. 90.

[9] See Kenneth Scott Latourette, *The Christian World Mission in Our Day* (New York: Harper & Brothers, 1954), pp. 101-102, 106; Stokes, *op. cit.*, Vol. I, Ch. 1, Sec. 4; Bates, *op. cit.*, Ch. 1; Brown, *op. cit., passim.*

[10] Matthew 22:21, Revised Standard Version. See Francis X. Curran, *The Churches and the Schools* (Chicago: Loyola Univ. Press, 1954), pp. 107-108, 115-116; Joseph Martin Dawson, *Separate Church and State Now* (New York: Richard R. Smith, 1948); David J. Brewer, *The United States, a Christian Nation* (Philadelphia: John C. Winston, 1905); Morton, *op. cit.*, pp. 163-166.

[11] See Henry P. Van Dusen, *God in Education* (New York: Charles Scribner's Sons, 1951), pp. 109 ff.; Frank Gavin, *Seven Centuries of the Problem of Church and State* (Princeton: Princeton Univ. Press, 1938), pp. 8-9.

[12] See H. M. J. Loewe, *Render Unto Caesar* (Cambridge Univ. Press, 1940), pp. 65-116; Heimann, *op. cit.*, pp. 215-216; *International Critical Commentary: Mark* (New York: Charles Scribner's Sons, 1913), pp. 226-227.

[13] Mark 2:27. See *Interpreter's Bible*, Vol. 7, p. 679.

[14] See *idem;* Niebuhr, *op. cit.*, p. 154.

[15] See Irwin, *op. cit.*, Ch. 7; Robert H. Pfeiffer, *Introduction to the Old Testament* (New York: Harper & Brothers, 1941), pp. 259-270; Troeltsch, *op. cit.*, Vol. 2, p. 586.

[16] See Fred L. Brownlee, *These Rights We Hold* (New York: Friendship Press, 1952), pp. 1-21; Cobb, *op. cit.*, Ch. 2; Troeltsch, *op. cit.*, Vol. 2, pp. 491-494, 653, 1007-1010; Gavin, *op. cit.*

[17] See Greene, *op. cit.*, Ch. 1; Brown, *op. cit.*, pp. 66 ff.; Cobb, *op. cit.*, Ch. 2; Troeltsch, *op. cit.*, Vol. 2, pp. 502-503, 519-521, 548-554; Gavin, *op. cit.;* Walker, *op. cit.*

[18] See Stokes, *op. cit.*, Vol. III, pp. 636-638; Bates, *op. cit.*, pp. 313-314; Brown, *op. cit., passim.*

[19] See Austin H. Burch, "Shall We Disestablish the Church?" *The Hibbert Journal*, Vol. 50, 1951-52, pp. 275-279; Bates, *op. cit.*, pp. 86-87.

[20] See Stokes, *op. cit.*, Vol. I, Ch. 3, Sec. 2; Greene, *op. cit.*, pp. 15, 21, 22, 32-46, 52; Bates, *op. cit.*, pp. 179-186, 216; Stumpf, *op. cit.*, pp. 134-135; Mecklin, *op. cit.*, Chs. 3, 4; Cobb, *op. cit., passim;* Sweet, *op. cit.*, Chs. 2, 3.

[21] It is true that the establishments in these three colonies were the most conspicuous, as scholarly studies bear out; see references for fn. 20, *supra.*

[22] See Greene, *op. cit.*, pp. 31-46; Sweet, *op. cit.*, pp. 28-29, 88-89; Stokes, *op. cit.*, Vol. I, Ch. 3, Sec. 2; Cobb, *op. cit.*, Ch. 4, Sec. 1, Ch. 5, Secs. 2, 3.

[23] See Greene, *op. cit.*, pp. 29-31, 61; Cobb, *op. cit.*, Ch. 6, Sec. 1; Sweet, *op. cit.*, pp. 35-39, 192-203, 206-209.

[24] See *ibid.*, pp. 33-35; Cobb, *op. cit.*, pp. 386 ff.; Greene, *op. cit.*, p. 64; Stokes, *op. cit.*, Vol. I, p. 194.

[25] See Cobb, *op. cit.*, Ch. 5, Sec. 5.

[26] See *ibid.*, Ch. 4, Sec. 2, Ch. 6, Sec. 4; Greene, *op. cit.*, p. 36; Sweet, *op. cit.*, pp. 39-45.

[27] See Cobb, *op. cit.*, Ch. 6, Secs. 2, 3; Ch. 7.

[28] See *idem;* Stokes, *op. cit.*, Vol. I, pp. 194, 274, 435, 857, 859; Greene, *op. cit.*, pp. 51, 58, 81; Bates, *op. cit.*, pp. 183-186, 216.

[29] See Rossiter, *op. cit.*, Ch. 7; Mecklin, *op. cit.*, Ch. 5; Sweet, *op. cit.*, pp. 122-127, 326-327; Cobb, *op. cit.*, pp. 423-436; Greene, *op. cit.*, pp. 43, 47-51; Stokes, *op. cit.*, Vol. I, pp. 194-205.

[30] See *ibid.*, Vol. I, pp. 380-392; Cobb, *op. cit.*, pp. 492-497.

[31] See Stokes, *op. cit.*, Vol. I, pp. 164, 387-389; Cobb, *op. cit.*, pp. 495-496.

[32] See Howe, *op. cit.*, pp. 5-7; Stokes, *op. cit.*, Vol. I, pp. 164, 341-344, 388-392; Cobb, *op. cit.*, pp. 496-497.

[33] See Stokes, *op. cit.*, Vol. I, pp. 392-394; Cobb, *op. cit.*, pp. 497-498.

[34] See Stokes, *op. cit.*, Vol. I, pp. 394-396; Cobb, *op. cit.*, pp. 498, 511-512.

[35] See Greene, *op. cit.*, p. 88; Stokes, *op. cit.*, Vol. I, pp. 336, 392.

[36] See Stokes, *op. cit.*, Vol. I, Ch. 5, Secs. 4, 5, 8; Cobb, *op. cit.*, pp. 499-507.

[37] See Howe, *op. cit.*, p. 84; Stokes, *op. cit.*, Vol. I, pp. 519-537, 540.

[38] See *ibid.*, Vol. I, pp. 527, 530, 531, 538, 539.

[39] See *ibid.*, Vol. I, pp. 537-541, 543-544, 553, 601-611.

[40] See *ibid.*, Vol. I, pp. 345, 541, 554; Wilfred Parsons, *The First Freedom* (New York: Declan X. McMullen, 1948), Ch. 3.

[41] See Stokes, *op. cit.*, Vol. I, pp. 540-549.

[42] The First Amendment begins: "Congress shall make no law respecting an establishment of religion, or prohibiting the free exercise thereof . . ." See *ibid.*, Vol. I, p. 548.

[43] See *ibid.*, Vol. I, pp. 408-427, 444, 553, 559, 576; Greene, *op. cit.*, pp. 84, 88-93; Cobb, *op. cit.*, pp. 512-515.

[44] See *supra*, p. 56, and Ch. 2, fn. 31.

[45] See Stokes, *op. cit.*, Vol. I, pp. 552-561; Morton, *op. cit.*, Ch. 1; Luther A. Weigle, "Freedom of Religion and Education," *Christianity and Crisis*, Vol. 10, No. 13 (July 24, 1950), pp. 98-103.

[46] See Sweet, *op. cit.*, Ch. 10; Rossiter, *op. cit.*, Ch. 2; Stokes, *op. cit.*, Vol. I, pp. 194-202, 208-216, 231, 244, 299-302, 306-310, 324-333, 353-355.

[47] See *ibid.*, Vol. I, pp. 293-299, 302-305, 310-318, 333-353, 508-514.

[48] See Bates, *op. cit.*, pp. 103-104, 193-198; Stokes, *op. cit.*, Vol. I, pp. 517, 647; Latourette, *A History of Christianity*, *op. cit.*, pp. 1093, 1109-1114.

[49] See Cobb, *op. cit.*, p. 497; Stokes, *op. cit.*, Vol. I, p. 341.

[50] See Royden J. Mott, "Sources of Jefferson's Ecclesiastical Views," *Church History*, Vol. 3, 1934, pp. 267-284; Stokes, *op. cit.*, Vol. I, pp. 336-339, 515-516; Henry Wilder Foote, *Thomas Jefferson, Champion of Religious Freedom, Advocate of Christian Morals* (Boston: Beacon Press, 1947).

[51] See Sweet, *op. cit.*, pp. 334-339; Rossiter, *op. cit.*, pp. 41-43.

[52] See Stokes, *op. cit.*, Vol. I, pp. 556, 780-783; Vol. III, p. 478; Winfred E. Garrison, "Social and Cultural Factors in Our Divisions," *Ecumenical Review*, Vol. 5, No. 1 (Oct. 1952), pp. 43-51.

[53] Quoted in Stokes, *op. cit.*, Vol. I, p. 418.

[54] See Luther A. Weigle, "Public Education and Religion," *Religious Education*, XXXV, 2 (Apr.-June, 1940), pp. 67-75; Arthur E. Sutherland, Jr., "Due Process and Disestablishment," *Harvard Law Review*, Vol. 62, No. 8 (June, 1949), pp. 1308-1309; Greene, *op. cit.*, pp. 96-98; Bates, *op. cit.*, pp. 529 ff.; Brewer, *op. cit.*; Stokes, *op. cit.*, Vol. I, pp. 517, 556; Vol. III, Ch. 24.

[55] See Sutherland, *op. cit.*, p. 1326; see also *infra*, pp. 131-142.

[56] Stokes, *op. cit.*, Vol. I, p. 47.

[57] *Idem.*

Chapter V. THE MISUNDERSTANDING OF RELIGIOUS FREEDOM

[1] See Annabelle Melville, *John Carroll of Baltimore: Founder of the American Catholic Hierarchy* (New York: Charles Scribner's Sons, 1955); Stokes, *op. cit.*, Vol. I, p. 90; Theodore Maynard, *The Story of American Catholicism* (New York: Macmillan, 1943), pp. 125-162.

[2] Stokes, *op. cit.*, Vol. I, p. 333. For John Carroll's influence, see *ibid.*, Vol. I, pp. 324-333, 800; Melville, *op. cit.*

[3] See Robert C. Hartnett, "The Religion of the Founding Fathers," in *Wellsprings of the American Spirit, op. cit.*, pp. 49-68; William Warren Sweet, *Religion in the Development of American Culture, 1765-1840* (New York: Charles Scribner's Sons, 1952), p. 49; Bates, *op. cit.*, p. 212; Stokes, *op. cit.*, Vol. I, pp. 88-91.

[4] See David S. Schaff, "The Bellarmine-Jefferson Legend and the Declaration of Independence," *Papers of the American Society of Church History*, Second Series, Vol. 8 (New York: G. P. Putnam's Sons, 1928), pp. 239-276; Sweet, *op. cit.*, pp. 49-50; Bates, *op. cit.*, pp. 212-214; Stokes, *op. cit.*, Vol. I, pp. 90-91.

[5] See Rossiter, *op. cit.*, pp. 136-137; Stokes, *op. cit.*, Vol. I, pp. 264-267; Latourette, *op. cit.*, pp. 1006-1007.

[6] See Rossiter, *op. cit.*, pp. 139-147, Chs. 12, 13, 14; Stokes, *op. cit.*, Vol. I, Ch. 4, Sec. 8; Charles A. and Mary Beard, *The Rise of American Civilization* (New York: Macmillan, 1942), Vol. I, pp. 237-240, 259-261.

[7] See *supra*, pp. 35, 98-99.

[8] See Aaron, *op. cit.*, pp. 295-306.

[9] See Nichols, *op. cit.*, p. 42; Stokes, *op. cit.*, Vol. I, pp. 265, 360-361, 553, 647; Vol. III, pp. 688-690; Beard and Beard, *op. cit.*, Vol. I, p. 360.

[10] See Rossiter, *op. cit.*, Ch. 5; Stokes, *op. cit.*, Vol. I, pp. 318-324, 333-350; Foote, *op. cit.*, p. 25.

[11] See Sweet, *op. cit.*, Ch. 1; Stokes, *op. cit.*, Vol. I, pp. 217-219, 279, 356.

[12] See Mecklin, *op. cit.*; Morton, *op. cit.*, Ch. 1; Rossiter, *op. cit.*, pp. 37-41, 44, 46-52, 56-58, 327-329; Sweet, *Religion in Colonial America*, pp. 322-333; Sweet, *Religion in the Development of American Culture*, Ch. 2; Stokes, *op. cit.*, Vol. I, pp. 219-222, 230-231, 235-238, 240-244, 356; Vol. III, p. 721; Luther A. Weigle, *American Idealism* (New Haven: Yale Univ. Press, 1928), pp. 122-123; Thomas Cuming Hall, *The Religious Background of American Culture* (Boston: Little, Brown, 1930).

[13] See Cobb, *op. cit.*, Ch. 4, Sec. 1; Mecklin, *op. cit.*, Chs. 10, 11; Stokes, *op. cit.*, Vol. I, pp. 208-216, 366-379.

[14] See Mecklin, *op. cit.*, pp. 274-277; Rossiter, *op. cit.*, p. 51; Sweet, *op. cit.*, Chs. 1, 2, *passim*; Stokes, *op. cit.*, Vol. I, pp. 366, 368, 611; Perry Miller, *op. cit.*

[15] See Bates, *op. cit.*, pp. 310-312; Stokes, *op. cit.*, Vol. I, pp. 230-231, 272-273, 611; Mecklin, *op. cit.*, *passim*.

[16] See Bates, *op. cit.*, pp. 89-95; Mecklin, *op. cit.*, Ch. 13; Stokes, *op. cit.*, Vol. I, p. 645; Rossiter, *op. cit.*, p. 41; Weigle, *op. cit.*, pp. 84-125.

[17] See Mecklin, *op. cit.*, Chs. 13, 14; Luther A. Weigle, *Religious Education*, Vol. 49, No. 2 (Mar.-Apr. 1954), p. 76; Stokes, *op. cit.*, Vol. I, pp. 230-231; Torpey, *op. cit.*, pp. 13 ff.

[18] *Everson v. Board of Education*, 330 U.S. 1.

[19] *Idem.*

[20] *Idem.*

[21] *Cochran v. Louisiania State Board of Education*, 281 U.S. 370.

[22] See Stokes, *op. cit.*, Vol. II, pp. 702-716; *Christian Century*, Vol. 64, No. 21 (May 21, 1947), pp. 652-653; Vol. 64, No. 50 (Dec. 10, 1947), pp. 1512-1514; R. Freeman Butts, *The American Tradition in Religion and Education* (Boston: Beacon Press, 1950), pp. 157-170; Leo Pfeffer, *Church, State, and Freedom* (Boston: Beacon Press, 1953), pp. 472-478; James M. O'Neill, *Religion and Education Under the Constitution* (New York: Harper & Brothers, 1949), Ch. 11.

[23] See *Christian Century, op. cit.*; Butts, *op. cit.*, p. 169; Pfeffer, *op. cit.*, pp. 472-478; Stokes, *op. cit.*, Vol. II, pp. 706, 709, 710, 712, 714.

[24] *McCollum v. Board of Education*, 333 U.S. 203. For discussions of the case, see Stokes, *op. cit.*, Vol. II, pp. 515-523; Sutherland, *op. cit.*, pp. 1311-1318; Vashti C. McCollum, *One Woman's Fight* (New York: Doubleday, 1951); *Christian Century*, Vol. 66, No. 23, pp. 707-709; Vol. 66, No. 24, pp. 734-737; Vol. 66, No. 25, pp. 760-763; Butts, *op. cit.*, pp. 201-208; Pfeffer, *op. cit.*, pp. 342-353; O'Neill, *op. cit.*, Ch. 12; Parsons, *op. cit.*, Ch. 11; *Law and Contemporary Problems*, Vol. 14, No. 1 (Winter, 1949).

[25] See Stokes, *op. cit.*, Vol. II, p. 522; Sutherland, *op. cit.*, p. 1315; F. Ernest Johnson, "Church, School, and Supreme Court," *Religion in Life*, Vol. 17, No. 4 (Autumn, 1948), p. 484.

[26] *McCollum v. Board of Education.*

[27] *Idem.*

[28] *Idem.*

[29] See O'Neill, *op. cit.*, p. 246.

[30] *McCollum v. Board of Education.*

[31] *Idem.*

[32] *Idem.*

[33] See Stokes, *op. cit.*, Vol. II, pp. 522-523, 535; National Education Association, *The Status of Religious Education in the Public Schools* (Washington: Research Division, N.E.A., 1949); Russell Sullivan, "Religious Education in the Schools," *Law and Contemporary Problems*, Vol. 14, No. 1 (Winter, 1949), pp. 92-112; Charles Clayton Morrison, "The Dissent of Mr. Justice Reed," *Christian Century*, Vol. 66, No. 25 (June 22, 1949), p. 761.

[34] See Sullivan, *op. cit.*, p. 109; Edward S. Corwin, "The Supreme Court as National School Board," *Law and Contemporary Problems*, Vol. 14, No. 1 (Winter, 1949), pp. 3-22.

[35] See Sutherland, *op. cit.*; John Courtney Murray, "Law or Prepossessions?" Alexander Meiklejohn, "Educational Cooperation Between

Church and State," and Charles Fahy, "Religion, Education, and the Supreme Court," *Law and Contemporary Problems*, Vol. 14, No. 1 (Winter, 1949), pp. 23-43, 61-91; *Christian Century*, Vol. 65, No. 14 (Apr. 7, 1948), pp. 308-309.

[36] See N.E.A., *op. cit.*; Stokes, *op. cit.*, Vol. II, pp. 522-523, 529; Pfeffer, *op. cit.*, pp. 351-353; Erwin L. Shaver, "Weekday Religious Education Is Now on Its Own," *International Journal of Religious Education*, Vol. 24, No. 10 (June, 1948), p. 5.

[37] *Zorach v. Clauson*, 343 U.S. 306.

[38] *Idem.*

[39] *Idem.*

Chapter VI.   THE PRICE OF MISUNDERSTANDING

[1] This statement is, of course, from a Protestant point of view, with the phrasing of which Catholics would quibble; but the reader can judge its soundness in the light of the voluminous Catholic and non-Catholic discussions of the Catholic positions on both theory and practice. See Bates, *op. cit.*, pp. 188-193, 324-330, 432-468; Stokes, *op. cit.*, Vol. I, Ch. 3, Sec. 1 (6); Vol. II, Ch. 19; Vol. III, Ch. 23, Sec. 4 (1); Greene, *op. cit.*, pp. 103-105; and references, *infra*, fn. 45; Christopher Dawson, *op. cit.*, Ch. 8; Charles C. Marshall, *The Roman Catholic Church in the Modern State* (New York: Dodd, Mead & Co., 1928), pp. 8, 15-56; and references, *supra*, Ch. 4, fns. 1, 2, and *infra*, fns. 10, 14, 15.

[2] Such efforts are usually on a local level and seldom receive national attention, but the Protestant press often reports incidents. For example, see *Christian Advocate*, Vol. 130, No. 24 (June 16, 1955), p. 4: "Father Harvey F. Egan of St. Mary's Catholic Church, Beardsley, Minn., population 500, protested when the school board decided to include a prayer in the high-school commencement. His letter stated, 'Catholics believe that the Catholic church is the one true church established by Jesus Christ . . . all other churches are false.' The board substituted a simple assembly." See also Stokes, *op. cit.*, Vol. II, p. 566; Greene, *op. cit.*, p. 124.

[3] See Stokes, *op. cit.*, Vol. II, pp. 544, 649; Paul Blanshard, *American Freedom and Catholic Power* (Boston: Beacon Press, 1949), pp. 79-82; William J. Butler, "No Lamb of God in School," *Catholic World*, Vol. 167, No. 999 (June, 1948), pp. 203-211; Charles Clayton Morrison, *Can Protestantism Win America?* (New York: Harper & Brothers, 1948), p. 66; David Schaff, *Our Fathers' Faith and Ours* (New York: G. P. Putnam Sons, 1928), p. 569.

[4] Both the extent and the limits of Catholic participation in such programs as released-time religious education and such organizations as the National Conference of Christians and Jews are well known. See Stokes, *op. cit.*, Vol. II, pp. 462-464, 545-547.

[5] See *ibid.*, Vol. II, p. 566; Sutherland, *op. cit.*, pp. 1313-1314, and his reference to *People ex rel. Ring v. Board of Education*, 245 Ill. 334; Parsons, *op. cit.*, pp. 64 ff.

[6] See Stokes, *op. cit.*, Vol. II, pp. 649, 658, 689-719, 754-756; Morrison, *op. cit.*, pp. 67-68.

[7] See Stokes, *op. cit.*, Vol. II, pp. 651-653; Vol. III, pp. 455-456; Morrison, *op. cit.*, pp. 67-68.

[8] See Thomas Sugrue, *A Catholic Speaks His Mind on America's Religious Conflict* (New York: Harper & Brothers, 1952); Stokes, *op. cit.*, Vol. III, pp. 457, 473-476, 479; Parsons, *op. cit.*, pp. 94-106; Theodore Maynard, *The Catholic Church and the American Idea* (New York: Appleton-Century-Crofts, 1953).

[9] See Stokes, *op. cit.*, Vol. II, pp. 589-591, 662-671; Blanshard, *op. cit.*, Ch. 5; Butts, *op. cit.*, Ch. 6; Pfeffer, *op. cit.*, Chs. 11, 12.

[10] John A. Ryan and Moorhouse F. X. Millar, *The State and the Church* (New York: Macmillan, 1936); Ryan and Francis J. Boland, *Catholic Principles of Politics* (New York: Macmillan, 1941).

[11] See Stokes, *op. cit.*, Vol. II, pp. 744-758; Pfeffer, *op. cit.*, pp. 486-494; *Commonweal*, Vol. 50, No. 17 (August 5, 1949), pp. 404-405; *Christian Century*, Vol. 66, No. 33 (August 17, 1949), pp. 955-956.

[12] See Sugrue, *op. cit.*, pp. 29, 31, 43, 53, 59; Stokes, *op. cit.*, Vol. III, pp. 457, 469 ff.; Luke Eugene Ebersole, *Church Lobbying in the Nation's Capital* (New York: Macmillan, 1951), Ch. 3, pp. 106-113, 170-175.

[13] See Sugrue, *op. cit.*, p. 53; James M. O'Neill, *Catholicism and American Freedom* (New York: Harper & Brothers, 1952) and *Catholics in Controversy* (New York: McMullen Books, 1954); J. E. Coogan, "That Wall of Separation," *Catholic World*, Vol. 172 (Jan. 1951), pp. 252-255; James M. Gillis, "No Time for Dissension," *Catholic World*, Vol. 172 (Dec. 1950), pp. 166-172; Reinhold Niebuhr, "The Rising Catholic-Protestant Tension," *Christianity and Crisis*, Vol. 9 (July 25, 1949), pp. 106-108.

[14] Parsons, *op. cit.*

[15] O'Neill, *Religion and Education Under the Constitution, op. cit.*, and *Catholicism and American Freedom, op. cit.* His *Catholics in Controversy*, *op. cit.*, is a recapitulation of his arguments and a stinging rejoinder to the critics of his position.

[16] O'Neill, *Religion and Education Under the Constitution, op. cit.*, p. 4. See also Parsons, *op. cit.*, Ch. 3.

[17] O'Neill, *op. cit.*, pp. 27-28, 100, 110-111, 252.

[18] Parsons, *op. cit.*, p. 162.

[19] *Ibid.*, pp. 80, 81. See also Ch. 9.

[20] *Ibid.*, Chs. 6 and 7.

[21] *Ibid.*, Ch. 8.

[22] *Ibid.*, p. 5.

[23] *Ibid.*, p. 146.

[24] O'Neill, *Religion and Education Under the Constitution, op. cit.*, p. 11. In his other two books he rehearses his argument; see *Catholicism and American Freedom, op. cit.*, Chs. 2, 3, 4; *Catholics in Controversy*, Ch. 3.

[25] O'Neill, *Religion and Education Under the Constitution, op. cit.*, p. 200.

[26] *Ibid.*, p. 235.

[27] *Ibid.*, p. 56.

[28] *Ibid.*, pp. 56-65, Chs. 5, 6, 7, 8, 9.

[29] *Ibid.*, p. 218.

[30] *Ibid.*, p. 21. See Ch. 2.

[31] He writes: ". . . these Justices of the Supreme Court apparently do not know the most important facts of our constitutional history. . . . The only other possibility is that they do know the facts but either callously ignore them, or wilfully misrepresent them." (*Ibid.*, p. 3.)

[32] *Ibid.*, p. 190.

[33] *Ibid.*, p. 3.

[34] *Ibid.*, pp. 3, 32.

[35] *Ibid.*, pp. 32, 33.

[36] *Ibid.*, pp. 10, 11.

[37] *Ibid.*, p. 11.

[38] *Ibid.*, p. 31.

[39] Frank Swancara, *Obstruction of Justice by Religion* (Denver: W. H. Courtright Pub. Co., 1936). See also his *The Separation of Religion and Government* (New York: Truth Seeker Co., 1950).

[40] B. H. Hartogensis, "Denial of Equal Rights to Religious Minorities and Non-Believers in the United States," *Yale Law Journal*, XXXIX (March, 1930), pp. 658-681.

[41] See Stokes, *op. cit.*, Vol. III, pp. 592-595; Swancara, *op. cit.*

[42] See Hocking, *op. cit.*, pp. 438 ff.; Stokes, *op. cit.*, Vol. III, pp. 369, 667; Cobb, *op. cit.*, p. 524; Wilber G. Katz, "The Freedom to Believe," *Atlantic*, Vol. 192, No. 4 (October, 1953), pp. 66-69.

[43] See Stokes, *op. cit.*, Vol. III, pp. 550-552, 595, 684; Cecil Northcott, "Christianity and Liberty," *Religion in Life*, Vol. 17, No. 2 (Spring, 1948), pp. 291-292.

[44] See Stokes, *op. cit.*, Vol. II, pp. 464-465, 713-715; Ebersole, *op. cit.*, pp. 67-73; *Christian Century*, Vol. 65, No. 3 (Jan. 21, 1948), pp. 79-82; Vol. 65, No. 7 (Feb. 18, 1948), pp. 198-200; *Information Service*, Vol. 27, No. 17 (April 24, 1948).

[45] Blanshard, *op. cit.*, and *Communism, Democracy, and Catholic Power* (Boston: Beacon Press, 1951); Butts, *op. cit.*; Joseph Martin Dawson, *op. cit.*, and *America's Way in Church, State and Society* (New York: Macmillan, 1953); Alvin W. Johnson, *The Legal Status of Church-State Relationships in the United States* (Minneapolis: Univ. of Minnesota Press, 1934) and Johnson and Frank H. Yost, *Separation of Church and State in the United States* (Minneapolis: Univ. of Minnesota Press, 1948); Conrad Henry Moehlman, *School and Church: The American Way* (New York: Harper & Brothers, 1944) and *The Wall of Separation Between Church and State* (Boston: Beacon Press, 1951); Leo Pfeffer, *op. cit.*; V. T. Thayer, *Religion in Public Education* (New York: Viking Press, 1947) and *The Attack Upon the American Secular School* (Boston: Beacon Press, 1951). See also Joseph L. Blau, *ed.*, *Cornerstones of Reli-*

gious Freedom in America (Boston: Beacon Press, 1949) for Blau's comments; and Milton R. Konvitz, "Separation of Church and State: The First Freedom," *Law and Contemporary Problems*, Vol. 14, No. 1 (Winter, 1949), pp. 44-60.

46 Butts, *op. cit.*, pp. xiii-xiv.
47 *Ibid.*, pp. 8-10. See also J. M. Dawson, *America's Way in Church, State and Society*, pp. 9, 29, 43; Thayer, *The Attack Upon the American Secular School*, pp. 88-90, 93, 95-98.
48 See Butts, *op. cit.*, pp. 68, 108-109; J. M. Dawson, *op. cit.*, p. 33; Pfeffer, *op. cit.*, p. 218.
49 See *supra*, p. 121.
50 Blanshard, *American Freedom and Catholic Power*, p. 286.
51 *Ibid.*, pp. 48-55.
52 *Ibid.*, p. 64.
53 *Ibid.*, pp. 89, 305. See also his *Communism, Democracy, and Catholic Power*, pp. 140-153, 226-227.
54 Johnson and Yost, *op. cit.*, p. 258.
55 *Idem.* See also Chs. 7, 8, 12, 13.
56 *Ibid.*, p. 258.
57 *Ibid.*, p. 260.
58 Alvin W. Johnson, *op. cit.*, p. 282.
59 Thayer, *op. cit.*, Chs. 2, 3, 5, 6, *passim.*
60 *Ibid.*, Ch. 4.
61 *Ibid.*, p. 79.
62 *Ibid.*, pp. 162-165, 177, 173-178.
63 *Ibid.*, p. 171.
64 *Ibid.*, p. 166. For Weigle's discussion, see *Religion and Public Education.*
65 Thayer, *op. cit.*, p. 166.
66 *Ibid.*, p. 207.
67 *Ibid.*, p. 203.
68 *Ibid.*, p. 236.
69 Moehlman, *The Wall of Separation Between Church and State*, pp. xiii, xiv, 54, 55, 67, 69, 80, 210; J. M. Dawson, *op. cit.*, pp. 26-29, 31, 33, 43.
70 *Ibid.*, p. 51.
71 Butts, *op. cit.*, Ch. 6, specifically pp. 146-186, 197-199.
72 *Ibid.*, Chs. 2, 3, pp. 119-130.
73 *Ibid.*, pp. 6-9.
74 *Ibid.*, p. 9.
75 *Ibid.*, p. 81.
76 *Ibid.*, p. 91.
77 *Ibid.*, p. 101.
78 *Idem.*
79 *Ibid.*, p. 108.
80 *Ibid.*, pp. 108-110, 150, 189-190, 210-212.

[81] Pfeffer, *op. cit.*, Chs. 6, 7, 8, 9, 10, 11, 12, 13.

[82] *Ibid.*, pp. 141-142.

[83] *Ibid.*, pp. 217-218.

[84] *Ibid.*, pp. 309-312.

[85] *Ibid.*, pp. 421-423.

[86] *Ibid.*, p. 604.

[87] *Ibid.*, p. 605.

[88] Bates, *op. cit.*; Brown, *op. cit.*; Corwin, *op. cit.*; Greene, *op. cit.*; Hocking, *op. cit.*; F. E. Johnson, *op. cit.*; Stokes, *op. cit.*; Sutherland, *op. cit.*; Sweet, *op. cit.*; Van Dusen, *op. cit.*; Weigle, *op. cit.* See also *Religion and Public Education;* William C. Bower, *Church and State in Education* (Chicago: Univ. of Chicago Press, 1944); Claud D. Nelson, *Church and State, The American Pattern of Interaction Between the Forces of Religion and of Government* (New York: N.C.C.C.U.S.A., 1953); Carl Zollmann, *American Church Law* (St. Paul: West Pub. Co., 1933); G. Elson Ruff, *The Dilemma of Church and State* (Philadelphia: Muhlenberg Press, 1954).

[89] *Zorach v. Clauson.*

[90] *Idem.*

[91] *Idem.*

Chapter VII.   "LET FREEDOM RING"

[1] See Ramsey, *op. cit.*, Ch. 9, sec. 4; Berggrav, *op. cit.*, pp. 300-319.

[2] See William Temple, *Christianity and Social Order* (New York: Penguin Books, 1942), pp. 8-10, and his *Essays in Christian Politics and Kindred Subjects* (London: Longmans, Green, 1927), pp. 19-31; Angus Dun, "The Social Responsibility of the Christian," in William Scarlett, ed., *Christianity Takes a Stand* (New York: Penguin Books, 1946), pp. 20-21; Stokes, *op. cit.*, Vol. III, pp. 671-676.

[3] Quoted in Hocking, *op. cit.*, pp. 435-436. See also Bates, *op. cit.*, p. 322.

[4] Quoted in Hocking, *op. cit.*, p. 436. See also Brown, *op. cit.*; Temple, *op. cit.*; Scarlett, *op. cit.*; Stokes, *op. cit.*, Vol. III, pp. 672-676; Greene, *op. cit.*, pp. 115 ff.; Ebersole, *op. cit.*; Hocking, *op. cit.*, pp. 436-443; W. A. Visser 't Hooft and J. H. Oldham, *The Church and Its Function in Society* (Chicago: Willett, Clark, 1937); J. Richard Spann, ed., *The Church and Social Responsibility* (Nashville: Abingdon-Cokesbury, 1953); John A. Hutchison, ed., *Christian Faith and Social Action* (New York: Charles Scribner's Sons, 1953).

[5] See Berggrav, *op. cit.*, Ch. 7; Nicholas Berdyaev, *Slavery and Freedom* (New York: Charles Scribner's Sons, 1944), pp. 59-72; Jacques Maritain, *Scholasticism and Politics* (New York: Macmillan, 1940), pp. 118-143; *Freedom and Authority in Our Time, Twelfth Symposium of the Conference on Science, Philosophy and Religion* (New York: Harper & Brothers, 1953).

[6] See Temple, *Christianity and Social Order*, pp. 10-23; John C. Bennett,

Christian Ethics and Social Policy (New York: Charles Scribner's Sons, 1946), Chs. 4, 5; 't Hooft and Oldham, *op. cit.*, pp. 200 ff.

[7] See Sutherland, *op. cit.*; Stokes, *op. cit.*, Vol. II, pp. 549, 553; Vol. III, p. 371; F. Ernest Johnson, "Policies and Practices of American Public Schools with Respect to Religion," *Religion and Public Education.*

[8] See Sutherland, *op. cit.*; Stokes, *op. cit.*, Vol. II, pp. 549-572; Ward W. Keesecker, *The Legal Status of Bible Reading and Religious Instruction in Public Schools* (Washington: Government Printing Office, 1930); Pfeffer, *op. cit.*, pp. 374-391; Johnson and Yost, *op. cit.*, Chs. 3, 4.

[9] Such statements are capable of almost endless documentation, illustrating both the offenses against freedom and their exposure. No good purpose is served by citing the nonfreedom literature; the following references are typical of writings that have exposed it or have protested against such influences: Elmer Davis, *But We Were Born Free* (Indianapolis: Bobbs-Merrill, 1954); Ben H. Bagdikian, *The Facts About Facts Forum* (Providence: Providence *Journal-Bulletin*, 1954); Ralph Lloyd Roy, *Apostles of Discord* (Boston: Beacon Press, 1953); "Loyalty in a Democracy," *Public Affairs Pamphlet*, No. 179; Alan Barth, *Loyalty of Free Men* (New York: Viking Press, 1951); Dan Gillmor, *Fear the Accuser* (New York: Abelard-Schuman, 1954); Ralph O'Leary, "The Minute Women," *Houston Post*, Oct. 11-28, 1953; Gordon D. Hall, *The Hate Campaign Against the U.N. One World Under Attack* (Boston: Beacon Press, 1952).

[10] See Trueblood, *op. cit.*, Ch. 6; Davis, *op. cit.*; Roy, *op. cit.*; Barth, *op. cit.*; Gillmor, *op. cit.*; "Loyalty in a Democracy," *op. cit.*; George Younger, "Protestant Piety and the Right Wing," *Social Action*, May 15, 1951.

[11] See G. Bromley Oxnam, *I Protest* (New York: Harper & Brothers, 1954).

[12] See David E. Lilienthal, *This I Do Believe* (New York: Harper & Brothers, 1949), pp. ix-xiii.

[13] Both Blanshard and O'Neill have been identified with such freedom-loving groups as the American Civil Liberties Union. Concern for freedom is evident in their writings; see Blanshard, *op. cit.*, *passim*, and O'Neill, *op. cit.*, *passim*.

[14] *United States v. Schwimmer.*

[15] Ralph O'Leary, in commenting on his articles concerning the Minute Women (see O'Leary, *op. cit.*), said: "In America, everybody should have the right to freedom. . . . I think the Minute Women had a perfect right to do what they did. But I just think people ought to know that they did it." ("The Houston Scare," *Time*, Vol. 62, No. 18, Nov. 2, 1953, pp. 49-51).

[16] See Davis, *op. cit.*; Trueblood, *op. cit.*; Ward, *op. cit.*; Learned Hand, *The Spirit of Liberty* (New York: Alfred A. Knopf, 1952); Charles W. Ferguson, *A Little Democracy Is a Dangerous Thing* (New York: Association Press, 1948); Stumpf, *op. cit.*; League of Women Voters, *Freedom*

Agenda (New York: Carrie Chapman Catt Memorial Fund, 1954); Francis Biddle, *The Fear of Freedom* (New York: Doubleday, 1951); Brownlee, *op. cit.*; Barth, *op. cit.*; Zechariah Chafee, Jr., "The Freedom to Think," *Atlantic*, Vol. 195, No. 1 (Jan. 1955), pp. 27-33; Perry Miller, Robert L. Calhoun, Nathan M. Pusey, and Reinhold Niebuhr, *Religion and Freedom of Thought* (New York: Doubleday, 1954); "Secrecy, Security, and Loyalty," *Bulletin of Atomic Scientists*, Vol. 11, No. 4 (April, 1955); "Freedom in America," *Southwest Review*, Vol. 38, No. 4 (Fall, 1953); *Freedom and Authority in Our Time.*

[17] See Stumpf, *op. cit.*, Ch. 6; Ward, *op. cit.*, Ch. 20; Barth, *op. cit.*, p. 3; Nels F. S. Ferré, "Authority and Freedom," in *Freedom and Authority in Our Time*, pp. 491-505.

Suggested Readings

An accounting of books, magazine articles, law cases, and other materials used in the preparation of the text is given in the footnotes. The following items are a selection of writings and law cases which will prove to be of special interest to those who wish to trace further any of the major theses here outlined.

AARON, R. I. *John Locke*. London: Oxford University Press, 1937.

BAINTON, ROLAND H. *The Travail of Religious Liberty*. Philadelphia: Westminster Press, 1951.

BARTH, ALAN. *Loyalty of Free Men*. New York: Viking Press, 1951.

BATES, M. SEARLE. *Religious Liberty: An Inquiry*. New York: International Missionary Council, 1945.

BENNETT, JOHN C. *Christian Ethics and Social Policy*. New York: Charles Scribner's Sons, 1946.

BERDYAEV, NICHOLAS. *Slavery and Freedom*. New York: Charles Scribner's Sons, 1944.

BERGGRAV, EIVIND. *Man and State*. Philadelphia: Muhlenberg Press, 1951.

BIDDLE, FRANCIS. *The Fear of Freedom*. New York: Doubleday, 1951.

BLANSHARD, PAUL. *American Freedom and Catholic Power*. Boston: Beacon Press, 1949.

——. *Communism, Democracy, and Catholic Power*. Boston: Beacon Press, 1951.

BLAU, JOSEPH L., ed. *Cornerstones of Religious Freedom in America*. Boston: Beacon Press, 1949.

BRANSCOMB, B. HARVIE. *The Teachings of Jesus*. Nashville: Cokesbury Press, 1931.

BROWN, WILLIAM ADAMS. *Church and State in Contemporary America*. New York: Charles Scribner's Sons, 1936.

Brownlee, Fred L. *These Rights We Hold*. New York: Friendship Press, 1952.

Brunner, Emil. *The Divine Imperative*. Philadelphia: Westminster Press, 1947.

Buck, Philo M., Jr. *Milton on Liberty*. Lincoln, Nebraska: University of Nebraska, 1925.

Butts, R. Freeman. *The American Tradition in Religion and Education*. Boston: Beacon Press, 1950.

The Catholic Church and Politics. Cambridge: Harvard Law School Forum, 1950.

Catholicism and America. New York: Harcourt, Brace, 1953.

Cobb, Sanford H. *The Rise of Religious Liberty in America*. New York: Macmillan, 1902.

Curran, Francis X. *The Churches and the Schools*. Chicago: Loyola University Press, 1954.

Davis, Elmer. *But We Were Born Free*. Indianapolis: Bobbs-Merrill, 1954.

Davis v. Beason, 133 U. S. 333.

Dawson, Christopher. *Religion and the Modern State*. New York: Sheed and Ward, 1937.

Dawson, Joseph Martin. *Separate Church and State Now*. New York: Richard R. Smith, 1948.

———. *America's Way in Church, State and Society*. New York: Macmillan, 1953.

Ebersole, Eugene. *Church Lobbying in the Nation's Capital*. New York: Macmillan, 1951.

Enslin, Morton Scott. *The Ethics of Paul*. New York: Harper & Brothers, 1930.

Everson v. Board of Education, 330 U.S. 1.

Foote, Henry Wilder. *Thomas Jefferson, Champion of Religious Freedom, Advocate of Christian Morals*. Boston: Beacon Press, 1947.

Freedom and Authority in Our Time. Twelfth Symposium of the Conference on Science, Philosophy and Religion. New York: Harper & Brothers, 1953.

"Freedom in America," *Southwest Review*. Vol. 38, No. 4, Fall, 1953.

GARRISON, WINFRED ERNEST. *A Protestant Manifesto*. Nashville: Abingdon Press, 1952.

GAVIN, FRANK. *Seven Centuries of the Problem of Church and State*. Princeton: Princeton University Press, 1938.

GILLMOR, DAN. *Fear the Accuser*. New York: Abelard-Shuman, 1954.

Girouard v. United States, 328 U.S. 61.

GOGUEL, MAURICE. *The Life of Jesus*. New York: Macmillan, 1933.

GREENE, EVARTS B. *Religion and the State*. New York: New York University Press, 1941.

HALL, THOMAS CUMING. *The Religious Background of American Culture*. Boston: Little, Brown, 1930.

HAND, LEARNED. *The Spirit of Liberty*. New York: Alfred A. Knopf, 1952.

HARDING, ARTHUR L., ed. *Origins of the Natural Law Tradition*. Dallas: Southern Methodist University Press, 1954.

HIEMANN, EDUARD. *Freedom and Order*. New York: Charles Scribner's Sons, 1947.

HOCKING, WILLIAM ERNEST. *Man and the State*. New Haven: Yale University Press, 1926.

HOWE, MARK DEWOLFE. *Cases in Church and State in the United States*. Cambridge: Harvard University Press, 1952.

HUTCHISON, JOHN A., ed. *Christian Faith and Social Action*. New York: Charles Scribner's Sons, 1953.

Interpreter's Bible. Nashville: Abingdon Press, 1953. Vols. VII, X.

IRWIN, WILLIAM A. *The Old Testament: Keystone of Human Culture*. New York: Henry Schuman, 1952.

JOHNSON, ALVIN W. *The Legal Status of Church-State Relationships in the United States*. Minneapolis: University of Minnesota Press, 1934.

———, AND YOST, FRANK H. *Separation of Church and State in the United States*. Minneapolis: University of Minnesota Press, 1948.

JOHNSON, F. ERNEST, ed. *American Education and Religion*. New York: Harper & Brothers, 1952.

———, ed. *Wellsprings of the American Spirit*. New York: Harper & Brothers, 1948.

KUHN, HELMUT. *Freedom Forgotten and Remembered*. Chapel Hill: University of North Carolina Press, 1943.

Late Corporation of the Church of Jesus Christ of Latter-Day Saints v. United States, 136 U. S. 1.

LATOURETTE, KENNETH SCOTT. *The Christian World Mission in Our Day*. New York: Harper & Brothers, 1954.

———. *A History of Christianity*. New York: Harper & Brothers, 1953.

Law and Contemporary Problems. Vol. 14, No. 1, Winter, 1949.

LEE, UMPHREY. *Render unto the People*. Nashville: Abingdon Press, 1947.

LILIENTHAL, DAVID E. *This I Do Believe*. New York: Harper & Brothers, 1949.

LOCKE, JOHN. *Of Civil Government*. London: J. M. Dent & Sons, 1924.

LOEWE, H. M. J. *Render Unto Caesar*. Cambridge University Press, 1940.

MANSON, THOMAS WALTER. *The Teaching of Jesus*. London: Cambridge University Press, 1931.

MARITAIN, JACQUES. *Scholasticism and Politics*. New York: Macmillan, 1940.

MARSHALL, CHARLES C. *The Roman Catholic Church in the Modern State*. New York: Dodd, Mead, 1928.

MARSHALL, JOHN S. *Hooker's Polity in Modern English*. Sewanee, Tenn.: University of the South Press, 1948.

MAYNARD, THEODORE. *The Catholic Church and the American Idea*. New York: Appleton-Century-Crofts, 1953.

MECKLIN, JOHN M. *The Story of American Dissent*. New York: Harcourt, Brace & Co., 1934.

Minersville School District v. Gobitis, 310 U.S. 586.

MOEHLMAN, CONRAD HENRY. *School and Church: The American Way*. New York: Harper & Brothers, 1944.

———. *The Wall of Separation Between Church and State*. Boston: Beacon Press, 1951.

MORRISON, CHARLES CLAYTON. *Can Protestantism Win America?* New York: Harper & Brothers, 1948.

MORTON, R. KEMP. *God in the Constitution*. Nashville: Cokesbury Press, 1933.

McCollum v. Board of Education, 333 U. S. 203.

NATIONAL EDUCATION ASSOCIATION. *The Status of Religious Educa-*

tion in the Public Schools. Washington: Research Division, N.E.A., 1949.

NELSON, CLAUD D. *Church and State, The American Pattern of Interaction Between the Forces of Religion and of Government.* New York: N.C.C.C.U.S.A., 1953.

NICHOLS, JAMES H. *Democracy and the Churches.* Philadelphia: Westminster Press, 1951.

NIEBUHR, REINHOLD. *The Children of Light and the Children of Darkness.* New York: Charles Scribner's Sons, 1944.

——. *An Interpretation of Christian Ethics.* New York: Harper & Brothers, 1935.

O'NEILL, JAMES M. *Catholicism and American Freedom.* New York: Harper & Brothers, 1952.

——. *Catholics in Controversy.* New York: McMullen Books, 1954.

——. *Religion and Education Under the Constitution.* New York: Harper & Brothers, 1949.

PARSONS, WILFRED. *The First Freedom.* New York: Declan X. McMullen, 1948.

PFEFFER, LEO. *Church, State, and Freedom.* Boston: Beacon Press, 1953.

RAMSEY, PAUL. *Basic Christian Ethics.* New York: Charles Scribner's Sons, 1951.

Religion and Public Education, American Council on Education Studies. IX, 22.

Reynolds v. United States, 98 U.S. 145.

ROSSITER, CLINTON. *Seedtime of the Republic.* New York: Harcourt, Brace & Co., 1953.

RUFF, G. ELSON. *The Dilemma of Church and State.* Philadelphia: Muhlenberg Press, 1954.

RUSSELL, JAMES E., ed. *National Policies for Education, Health and Social Services.* Garden City: Doubleday, 1955.

RYAN, JOHN A., AND BOLAND, FRANCIS J. *Catholic Principles of Politics.* New York: Macmillan, 1941.

SCOTT, R. B. Y. *The Relevance of the Prophets.* New York: Macmillan, 1947.

STOKES, ANSON PHELPS. *Church and State in the United States.* New York: Harper & Brothers, 1950.

STUMPF, SAMUEL E. *A Democratic Manifesto*. Nashville: Vanderbilt University Press, 1954.

SUGRUE, THOMAS. *A Catholic Speaks His Mind on America's Religious Conflict*. New York: Harper & Brothers, 1952.

SUTHERLAND, ARTHUR E., JR. "Due Process and Disestablishment," *Harvard Law Review*. Vol. 62, No. 8, June, 1949.

SWEET, WILLIAM WARREN. *Religion in Colonial America*. New York: Charles Scribner's Sons, 1942.

———. *Religion in the Development of American Culture, 1765–1840*. New York: Charles Scribner's Sons, 1952.

TEMPLE, WILLIAM. *Christianity and Social Order*. New York: Penguin Books, 1942.

———. *Essays in Christian Politics and Kindred Subjects*. London: Longmans, Green & Co., 1927.

THAYER, V. T. *Religion in Public Education*. New York: Viking Press, 1947.

———. *The Attack upon the American Secular School*. Boston: Beacon Press, 1951.

'T HOOFT, W. A. VISSER, and OLDHAM, J. H. *The Church and Its Function in Society*. Chicago: Willett, Clark & Co., 1937.

TORPEY, WILLIAM GEORGE. *Judicial Doctrines of Religious Rights in America*. Chapel Hill: University of North Carolina Press, 1948.

TROELTSCH, ERNST. *The Social Teaching of the Christian Churches*. New York: Macmillan, 1950.

TRUEBLOOD, ELTON. *Declaration of Freedom*. New York: Harper & Brothers, 1955.

United States v. Macintosh, 283 U. S. 605.

WARD, BARBARA. *Faith and Freedom*. New York: W. W. Norton & Co., 1954.

West Virginia State Board of Education v. Barnette, 319 U.S. 624.

ZOLLMANN, CARL. *American Church Law*. St. Paul: West Publishing Company, 1933.

Zorach v. Clauson, 343 U.S. 306.

Index